D0428075

L.A. Story
and
Roxanne

L.A. Story

and

Roxanne

Two Screenplays

by Steve Martin

Grove Press
New York

Published simultaneously in Canada
Printed in the United States of America

FIRST EDITION

Library of Congress Cataloging-in-Publication Data
Martin, Steve, 1945–
    [L.A. story]
    L.A. story ; and, Roxanne : two screenplays / by Steve Martin. —
1st ed.
        p. cm.
    ISBN 0–8021–3512–9
    I. Martin, Steve, 1945– Roxanne.   II. L.A. story (Motion
picture)   III. Roxanne (Motion picture)   IV. Title.   V. Title:
Roxanne.
PN1997.L118   1997
791.43'75—dc21
                                                                    97–1597
                                                                    CIP
Design by Laura Hammond Hough

Grove Press
841 Broadway
New York, NY 10003

10 9 8 7 6 5 4 3 2 1

Acknowledgments

The author wishes to thank Victoria Tennant, Daniel Melnick, Carl Reiner, Fred Schepisi, and Mick Jackson for their help, guidance, understanding, and contributions to these screenplays.

L.A. Story

The cast of L.A. Story *includes:*

Harris	Steve Martin
Sara	Victoria Tennant
Roland	Richard E. Grant
Trudi	Marilu Henner
SanDee	Sarah Jessica Parker
Ariel	Susan Forristal
Frank Swan	Kevin Pollak
Morris Frost	Sam McMurray
Directed by	Mick Jackson
Screenplay by	Steve Martin
Director of Photography	Andrew Dunn
Edited by	Richard A. Harris
Music by	Peter Melnick
Production Designer	Lawrence Miller
Produced by	Daniel Melnick and Michael Rachmil

EXT. SKY—DAY

An airplane lands at LAX. Pan down to a billboard of the sun-baked body of a bikini-clad girl.

TITLE CARD: LOS ANGELES

THEN: TEMPERATURE, 71

A hot dog stand in the shape of a hot dog moves across the frame, suspended from chains attached to a helicopter. We follow it across the Los Angeles horizon. Finally, the hot dog stand is lowered into place on the above billboard advertising hot dogs.

MONTAGE—LOS ANGELES

At its best: smogless skies, clear freeways, the beach, a woman's behind in jeans that we find out is a man's. Beverly Hills mansions, etc., mixed in with the weird structures like houses in West Hollywood, and fuzzy '56 Plymouths. Sunrises, sunsets, palms.

EXT. POOL—DAY

A girl dives silently into a swimming pool.

EXT. STREET—DAY

Driveways jut out in front of their houses in perfect symmetry. In slow motion the occupants simultaneously appear out of their front doors and balletically retrieve the morning papers, in perfect time with the music.

EXT. STREET—DAY

We see a parking sign that reads, "Libra Parking Only." A beautifully coiffured guy slips his car perfectly into the space, while teasing his hair in the rearview mirror.

EXT. STREET—DAY

A traffic light at a crosswalk reads, "UH, LIKE WALK," then changes to "UH, LIKE DON'T WALK."

EXT. CURB—DAY

A man stops at a curb. A valet parker grabs his car. The man walks up to a coin-operated newspaper bin, gets a paper, and hands his ticket back to the valet parker.

EXT. STREET—DAY

A four-way stop, shot from overhead. A car waiting at each sign. They simultaneously start across the intersection and smash into each other.

EXT. STREET—DAY

Construction site. A sign reads, "To be built on this site, The Ugliest Fucking Building You've Ever Seen."

EXT. FREEWAY—DAY

The digital freeway condition sign. It reads, "Clear Sailing." The freeway is wide open.

EXT. STREET—DAY

A street musician plays the electric guitar for money. We follow the cord around the block to see it's connected to a bank of generators and recording equipment manned by all-pro operators.

EXT. JUNKYARD—DAY

One of those car dumps where hundreds of squashed cars sit on top of one another. There's a twenty-year-old kid in front in a uniform. The sign above reads, "Val's Gourmet Airport Parking, 50 Cents."

EXT. RESIDENTIAL NEIGHBORHOOD—DAY

A man in beach gear and sandals walks down the sidewalk with a Christmas tree under his arm.

EXT. BEVERLY HILLS—DAY

Flat-chested women go into a medical building while women with large breasts exit.

EXT. HOUSE—DAY

An elderly man hobbles out of a building using a walker. He approaches an open-top Italian automobile parked in a handicapped zone. He looks around furtively, tosses his walker in the back of his car, and spryly gets in.

EXT. LOS ANGELES PARK—DAY

We are tight on the face of HARRIS K. TELEMACHER. He is outdoors, exercising.

> HARRIS (*voice-over*)
> My name is Harris K. Telemacher. I live in Los
> Angeles and I've had seven heart attacks . . . all
> imagined. That is to say, I was deeply unhappy, but
> I didn't know it because I was so happy all the
> time . . . that is to say, if I hadn't met her, I
> wouldn't have known how lucky I was to have met
> her. I hope I didn't confuse you. Anyway, this is
> what happened to me, and I swear it's all true.

THREE QUICK CUTS

We see he is on a stationary bike, pedaling fiercely.

Wider, we see his bike is on a jogging track with fifteen or so other stationary bike riders.

Wider again, we see the entire picture: a jogging track with the stationary bike riders (with a few men on rowing machines), pedaling away under the Los Angeles sun and a sign in the foreground saying, "Stationary Bike Riding Park, gift of Shore, Davis, Manella, Seton and Fenner" and then underneath, "No Running."

EXT. HARRIS'S APARTMENT—DAY

He gets in his Honda and backs it into the street.

INT. HARRIS'S CAR—DAY

The radio voice says, ". . . Heavy traffic all over town today."
HARRIS makes a mental note, and a quick turn with the car.

EXT. STREETS—DAY

MONTAGE

HARRIS drives up his neighbor's driveway.

He drives across their backyard and out a gate.

In an alley, he makes a right into a stand of bushes.

Across another yard and off the curb, into a parking garage.

Out the other end of the parking garage and across a strand of
lawns on a traffic-jammed street.

Into the L.A. River.

Out the river and across a garbage dump.

Through a park and up one of the Hollywood Hills.

Over a high curb ending up in the parking lot of Sunumono
Broadcasting, Inc.

He parks in his spot and checks his watch.

Out of his car, he looks up at the sky and makes some notes.

INT. TV STUDIO—DAY

HARRIS and FRANK SWAN, his agent, are walking down a hall.

                    FRANK
     Well, why not? You've got to keep moving, be out
     there, be seen, and this is a perfect opportunity. As
     your agent I've got to advise you . . .

HARRIS

I can't be in a parade! I'm in the news. You won't
see Dan Rather or Diane Sawyer in the Hollywood
Day Parade. What good will it do me to stand in a
convertible and wave at people?

FRANK

It will make you beloved.

HARRIS

Waving is not what I do best. It always looks fake.
(*He demonstrates.*) Look, I've got to maintain
some dignity. People have to respect me so they'll
believe what I tell them. This is news. This is truth.

VOICE

Five seconds, Harris.

HARRIS

Right. Did you hear what the weather's supposed
to be like tomorrow?

FRANK

Sunny, warm.

They turn a corner into a TV studio.

On the countdown, "three . . . two . . . one . . . ," he jumps in
front of the TV cameras to take his position in front of a weather
map.

HARRIS (*into camera*)

HEY, HEY, HEY! It's time for the WAC WAC
WACKY weekend weather! Sunny and warm
tomorrow!

He takes a drink from a drinking glass and spits it out on the
floor.

HARRIS

Okay, here's the report: Today Muggy, followed
by Toogy, Wiggy and Thurggy. Seriously, Tues-
day, 72, Wednesday, 72, Thursday, watch out, 73,
Friday, whew, 72 again. Saturday is your mystery
day . . . maybe rain, maybe sun. . . . Sunday . . .
watch out . . . 72 again . . . surprise.

He points to weather map and moves plastic clouds all over it.
Half of the clouds fall on the floor.

HARRIS (*continuing*)

Here we have a low pushing out the high and
here's that high we talked about moving up to the
higher yet lower pressure area.

The map falls down with all its stuff, revealing a backdrop that
says, "Genuine Asbestos."

HARRIS

Got it? And now the Car Phone report.

A little phone logo pops on a corner of the screen.

HARRIS

Sunspot activity is at a minimum so those with car
phones will have no interference, although driving
through the canyons is always bad so be extra
careful not to make important calls there because
there's a good chance of being disconnected. And
that's the weather.

The other newspersons overlaugh hysterically. The FEMALE NEWS
REPORTER, who's more serious, speaks to HARRIS.

FEMALE NEWS REPORTER

Harris, someone told me you have a Ph.D. in Arts
and Humanities. . . .

HARRIS

Yes, I do.

FEMALE NEWS REPORTER

Lot of good it did you.

On Harris's look we cut.

INT. TV STUDIO—DAY

Harris's boss, TOD, much younger than he, is talking to HARRIS.

TOD

Harris, Harris. What's wacky?

HARRIS

What's wacky?

TOD

What's wacky about your last weather forecast?

HARRIS

It was pretty wacky.

TOD

Uh uh. No. Not wacky.

HARRIS

Not wacky?!!!

HARRIS emits a sarcastic guffaw. TOD is interrupted by a FEMALE
EMPLOYEE holding up two drawings.

GIRL

This or this?

TOD

That. (*To Harris.*) That's what we bought with you.
You're doing some kind of intellectual stuff out
there.

During Harris's next speech, a male worker asks TOD if they
want to go with the Milli Vanelli piece. TOD says, "After the train
crash piece, remember, alternate the stories, tragic, light, tragic,
light."

HARRIS

Intellectual stuff? Maybe intellectual to you,
because you were educated with a banana and an
inner tube. Are you kidding? This is an intellectual
free zone.

TOD

More wacky, less egghead.

He takes out his portable electronic note taker.

HARRIS

Let me just jot that down, more wacky, less egghead. And what was your name again?

INT. TRUDI'S APARTMENT—DAY

A nice Westwood apartment, walking distance to the village. We
hear sounds of someone moving around in the bathroom. He
rises and crosses to the hall door.

HARRIS (*trying to get her moving*)

We're late, aren't we?

TRUDI sticks her head out of the bedroom. She's early thirties,
stylish, but slightly too Gucci, slightly too "done up."

                              TRUDI
It's only one o'clock.

She ducks back in the bathroom.

                              HARRIS
That's what time we're supposed to be there. It's
my mistake. If I say the lunch is at one, I figure if I
pick you up at 12:40, we'll get there on time.
Which is fine. But what I don't count on is the
twenty minutes of . . . abstract "busyness" that goes
on after I get here.

                              TRUDI
They can wait; it's not going to kill them. I'm
doing thirty-minute lips!

                              HARRIS
The part that I can't figure is that you look ready.
In fact, you look so ready that I get ready and I get
my keys out and kind of stand by the door and
you're just about ready and then after I stand there
about ten minutes I realize you're not ready so I sit
down. Then I get another feeling that you're ready
and I get up and straighten my tie and then I
realize you just gave off an illusion of being ready
that I interpreted as not being an illusion. I'll be in
the car.

EXT. DRIVEWAY—DAY
HARRIS is in the car. He can see into the open door of the apartment and TRUDI is on her way. He starts up the engine. But she
waits by the passenger door, making him get out and open it
for her.

EXT. CAR—DRAMATIC SHOTS—SANTA MONICA FREEWAY—DAY

The car is mounting the freeway. The dialogue continues over shots of the freeway, including the digital warning sign of traffic ahead, which reads, "No Delays."

TRUDI (*v.o.*)

You really are L.A.

HARRIS (*v.o.*)

How's that?

TRUDI (*v.o.*)

You wear sunglasses on cloudy days.

HARRIS (*v.o.*)

That's because of the L.A. light. . . .

TRUDI (*v.o.*)

You blow-dry your hair.

HARRIS (*v.o.*)

I don't blow-dry my hair, I dry it with a blower.
There's a difference. I don't puff it up or anything.
And you can't tell me they're not blow-drying in
Kansas or New York or Panama. I'll bet Noriega
blow-dries. They might not let on like they're
blow-drying it, but I guarantee you they are.
I'm not L.A.

TRUDI

You are.

HARRIS

I'm not. I've never even felt euphoria while
exercising.

INT. CAR—DAY

They continue driving. The radio is on. They pass another free-way sign. This one, curiously enough, has a man standing in front of it.

VOICE ON RADIO

. . . and if you sense something funny in the air, it's not smog, it's because it's the first day of spring. . . .

HARRIS

What did he say?

TRUDI

He said it's the first day of spring. . . .

HARRIS

Oh shit. . . .

TRUDI (*nervous about something*)

God. You're the meteorologist. You're supposed to know it's the first day of spring.

HARRIS

I'm not a meteorologist, I'm a funny weatherman. There's a big difference. A meteorologist gets to go to school and study. I have to get up and do it with no knowledge of the weather at all.

Reaching under his car seat, he produces a 45-caliber handgun, which he proceeds to load. He speaks as he loads it.

TRUDI

Hurry. . . .

He finishes loading it. His car swerves a bit, which forces a pickup truck to slow. The DRIVER, angry, leans out the window.

13

DRIVER

. . . You son of a bitch!

The DRIVER pulls out his own gun and begins to fire. HARRIS fires
back. There is a little gun play but HARRIS turns the corner and
escapes.

Turning the corner, he inadvertently cuts off another car. This
time it's an OLDER WOMAN in a Mercedes. She pulls a weapon and
starts firing.

WOMAN

Ya little cocker. . . !

HARRIS fires back, no real aiming, just another day in Los Angeles.

EXT. STREET—DAY

They park and HARRIS hurriedly gets out of the car and walks
quickly toward the restaurant. After about fifty paces of brisk
walking and talking, he realizes that TRUDI is in the car waiting
for him to open the door. He darts back to do his manly duty.

HARRIS

Who are these people again?

TRUDI

Friends and friends of friends. And some of my gift-
service clients. Frank will be there.

HARRIS

Frank? I just saw Frank. He truly does not qualify as
an agent. If it wasn't impossible for me to fire
people, I'd get somebody else.

TRUDI

Frank's got tons of commercial auditions for you.

HARRIS

What does he do, call you and complain about
me? You know what one commercial was for?
Older guy jeans, "with a skosh more room." I'm
not ready for that. . . . I'm only thirty or forty,
something like that.

TRUDI

Tom Wells will be here, too.

HARRIS

Oh shit, the one who's a . . . what's he call it?

TRUDI

Interior plant designer.

HARRIS

Interior plant designer. What's his girlfriend's
name?

TRUDI

Oh God, either Shelly or Shirley. . . . She's a
fashion faux pas; she's really a stupid girl.

HARRIS

How do you know she's stupid?

TRUDI

From the way she dresses.

HARRIS

I think your argument is circular. Sheila! . . . That's
her name. She's the one who's always kissing
everybody hello. God, I hate that. I'm not kissing
anyone anymore. That's it.

EXT. RESTAURANT—DAY

The MAITRE D' greets them.

MAITRE D'

Yes, you're the first ones to arrive.

TRUDI scowls at him.

INT. RESTAURANT—DAY

They sit at the solitary table. Then, everyone starts arriving. Saturday brunch, table for eight. HARRIS enthusiastically shakes hands with FRANK, his hyperenergetic agent, and plants a triple kiss on each cheek of his date, SHEILA. Next, it's MORRIS FROST, a television movie reviewer, with a great-looking girl. There is a handsome Englishman, ROLAND DRAKE.

MORRIS

Hi, Harris. . . .

They shake.

HARRIS

You remember Trudi. . . .

MORRIS

Of course. . . .

They kiss.

TRUDI

Hi. . . .

HARRIS (*to Trudi*)

This is Morris Frost and of course you remember . . .

HARRIS has a big scary moment of memory loss. Another couple, TOM (the interior plant designer) and SHEILA, join them. SHEILA is dressed like a gaucho (you've seen them).

TOM

Hi, Morris . . . Cynthia . . . !

HARRIS

. . . Cynthia.

TOM

I have to stand during lunch; I hurt my back at tennis. . . .

CYNTHIA

(*Kissing Trudi.*) Hi, Trudi . . . (*Kissing Harris.*) Hi, Harris. . . .

Another couple arrives at the table, TED and SHARON. SHARON is wearing a large bandage over her nose and TED is dressed in a cop's uniform. We dissolve with everyone kissing and shaking hands, especially HARRIS.

LATER IN THE LUNCH

TOM (the one who hurt his back) stands through the entire meal. Everyone's gabbing animatedly.

MORRIS

So I see the film and I'm going to give it an eight or a seven, I don't know. But as I'm leaving the parking lot, I realize that Thurlow, the producer, has this incredible reserved parking space right next to the entrance and they gave me a lousy place in the far end. So I go on that night and give it a three.

LATER IN THE LUNCH
TRUDI introduces SHEILA to HARRIS.

TRUDI

Sheila has been taking a course in the art of conversation.

HARRIS

So you've been studying the art of conversation. . . .

SHEILA

Yes.

Silence.

LATER IN THE LUNCH
SHARON takes out a cigarette and starts to light it.

SHARON

Whatever you do, don't get dumped in L.A. In New York, you can always meet someone walking down the street. In L.A. you can only meet someone if you hit them with your car. Which some people do intentionally. I know girls who speed just to meet cops.

TED

We met on a hit in West Hollywood.

SHEILA, about to light her cigarette, is frowned upon by everyone at the lunch. She puts the cigarette away.

LATER IN THE LUNCH

TOM (*standing*)
. . . Loud talkers in restaurants; they're driving me crazy! What can we do about them?

A pretty, blond English girl, mid-thirties, joins the table and sits at the far end away from HARRIS. She is SARA MCDOWEL. There is a round of hellos and introductions to HARRIS and TRUDI and she sits next to ROLAND DRAKE.

                    ROLAND
Sara just got off a plane from London.

                    MORRIS
You must be exhausted.

                    SARA
Nothing that some sleep and a good fuck
wouldn't cure.

She bursts into a giggle, surprised that she would say such a thing. Everyone stares.

                    ROLAND
You have to forgive Sara; she has a bad family
gene. She tries to suppress it but sometimes things
just fly out.

                    SARA
Sorry. I've been on a plane for twelve hours next to
a crying infant.

                    SHARON
How old?

                    SARA
Mid- to late forties.

                    MORRIS
What do you give the flight?

SARA

What?

MORRIS

You know, on a scale of one to ten.

SARA

I really don't know. What kind of food do they have here?

EVERYONE ALMOST SIMULTANEOUSLY (*boasting*)

California cuisine.

LATER IN THE LUNCH

TOM (*standing*)

. . . these goddam wrong-number dialers! What in hell are we going to do about them?

MORRIS

. . . So everybody kept saying, "Go to Spain, go to Spain . . . it's great." We go. I give it a five.

FRANK

What do you do, Sara?

SARA

I'm writing an article about Los Angeles for the *London Times*.

HARRIS

Well, you've come to the right place.

An earthquake. Everyone keeps talking as if nothing is happening.

ROLAND

You know what they say about L.A. "It's not the
heat, it's the stupidity."

Polite laughter.

TOM

What do you do, Roland?

ROLAND

I deal in English paintings.

FRANK

Abstract or realistic?

ROLAND

Depends on which way you hang them I suppose. . . . What's that?

MORRIS

Earthquake. How strong is it, Harris?

A party of four slides across the room behind them.

HARRIS

I give it a four.

SARA

Should we be worried?

LATER IN THE LUNCH

TRUDI (*to Sara*)

. . . so when an executive needs a gift for someone,
my company picks something out that's appropriate.

SARA

You mean you pick out gifts for someone to give other people?

TRUDI

I gifted Sherman, Lee and Rosenquist's entire office last Christmas.

SARA mouths to herself, "Gifted," to remember it.

SARA

"Gifted" sounds very L.A.

TRUDI

It's not. Did you know it's been going on since Alexander the Great? Let me give you my card.

ROLAND

I think I received something from them last Christmas. A stun gun.

TRUDI

That was me.

SARA starts giggling to the point that she's noticed. She fiddles looking for a hanky in her purse. We see glimpses of odd items: something brass, a boccie ball, a half blown-up balloon. We see a couple in the background in a wedding dress and morning coat, obviously just married, ordering lunch.

MORRIS

She ought to interview Harry Zell.

TED

Who's Harry Zell?

MORRIS

Harry Zell is the most powerful show business
agent in town.

FRANK

Beyond powerful. The fixer. The miracle worker.

TRUDI

He's supposed to be nice.

FRANK (*meaning it*)

He's a guy who would never stab you in the back
unless it was in self-defense.

SARA spills water on her dress. HARRIS offers her his napkin. She
waves it off.

SARA

I keep thinking I'm a grown-up but I'm not.

She looks at him and hiccups.

LATER IN THE LUNCH

TOM

I'll have a decaf coffee.

TRUDI

I'll have a decaf espresso.

MORRIS

I'll have a double decaf cappuccino.

TED

Do you have any decaffeinated coffee ice cream?

HARRIS

I'll have a half-double decaffeinated half-caf. With
a twist of lemon.

TOM

I'll have a twist of lemon.

TRUDI

I'll have a twist of lemon.

MORRIS

I'll have a twist of lemon.

TED

I'll have a twist of lemon.

LUNCH IS OVER

Everyone stands up with their good-byes.

HARRIS (*to the group*)

I really enjoyed myself. And I enjoyed all of you,
too.

TRUDI scowls. No one finds this funny, absolutely no one. Except
for SARA. TRUDI mentions to SARA, "I would love to do a makeover
on you." As the parties rise, HARRIS finds himself near SARA and, as
a waiter crosses her path, he takes her elbow and moves her
out of the way.

EXT. STREET—DAY

HARRIS and TRUDI are walking back to the car.

TRUDI

Wasn't that girl Sara awful? What was that she was
wearing?

HARRIS

It's better than dressing like a gaucho.

TRUDI

She's a glamour Don't. And what's with that
accent? Ugh.

ANGLE ON SARA AND ROLAND

SARA and ROLAND finishing coffee.

SARA

I liked that girl Trudi. She seemed to be a very kind
person.

ROLAND

Who was she with?

SARA

She was with that agent, Frank, wasn't she? She
had a very sweet quality.

ANGLE ON HARRIS AND TRUDI

HARRIS and TRUDI walking to the car.

TRUDI

She talks that way just to impress everybody.

HARRIS

Oh, you mean like that big phoney Winston
Churchill.

ANGLE ON ROLAND AND SARA

ROLAND

So, Sara, about what you said in there . . . about
some sleep and a good . . .

SARA

Oh god! What is wrong with me? If I do it again,
tie me up and gag me.

ROLAND

I believe we tried that once but you started laughing. You sleep and we'll see each other tomorrow.
. . . Sara, what are our chances?

SARA

Roland, I'm completely happy with the way things
are now. I've finally settled into a peaceful life.

ROLAND

Well, maybe L.A. will shake it up a little.

ANGLE ON TRUDI AND HARRIS

TRUDI

She's not one of us.

HARRIS

I don't think you understand how unattractive hate
is.

He fiddles with his keys to open the car. At that moment, SARA
yells at them from her car across the street as ROLAND drives off.

SARA

Excuse me, can you help me?

HARRIS

Sure.

SARA

Do people get up early or late here?

                                    HARRIS
It depends. Why?

                                     SARA
Well, if a person were to be making a lot of noise,
what time could they start?

                                    HARRIS
What kind of noise? Like construction?

                                     SARA
No, more like deep sustained booming sounds.

TRUDI gives a mortified look to HARRIS.

                                    HARRIS
Deep, sustained, booming sounds? Around 9:00,
9:15.

                                     SARA
Thank you.

The bride and groom from the restaurant kiss and fall over a
hedge into the bushes.

SARA gets in her car, pulls out, and drives for about a block on
the left-hand side of the street. HARRIS watches in amazement.
She swerves back into the right-hand lane at the last minute.
HARRIS gets in the car and starts to drive away, leaving TRUDI at
the curb.

                                     TRUDI
HEY!!!

He pulls back in the space, gets out, goes around, and opens
the car door for her.

                                       27

INT. FRED SEGAL'S CLOTHING STORE—DIFFERENT DAY

TRUDI is shopping as HARRIS watches. HARRIS wanders off and finds himself in another part of the store. The store is active, both men and women trying things on. HARRIS is trying on pants. We catch HARRIS glimpsing skirts falling behind the dressing room doors. One door is open slightly too much, seeing a little bra and panties, proof that clothing stores are the sexiest places in Los Angeles. A female clerk, SANDEE, twenty-two, bouncy and openly friendly, approaches him. He just glimpses a girl button up her blouse.

                    SANDEE
Do you like those?

                    HARRIS (*caught*)
Huh?

                    SANDEE
Your pants. Shall I mark 'em for you?

                    HARRIS
I don't know. Are these the same price as the other ones?

                    SANDEE
They're a little more.

                    HARRIS
How do they look?

She stands back and looks him up and down.

                    SANDEE
You look fabulous in those.

                         HARRIS
Okay, mark 'em.

SANDEE kneels down, her slightly loose blouse hanging slightly
open, and spends several minutes adjusting the pants.

                         SANDEE
Stand up straight or they won't be right. Do you
like a break?

                         HARRIS
A little.

                         SANDEE
Like that?

                         HARRIS
That's fine.

She starts to pin them. This makes her bend further over and
HARRIS tries to watch and not watch at the same time.

                         SANDEE
Okay.

She bounces up.

                         HARRIS
When can I get these?

                         SANDEE
Just any time you want. Wednesday okay?

She leads him over to the tie display. She shows him a pretty
wild punk sort of fluorescent thing. She lays the tie against his
shirt.

                           29

SANDEE (*continuing*)
It's great, isn't it? It looks good on you.

They are now at the counter, HARRIS paying for his goods. She hands him a sack and a ticket for his pants and, at the same time, gives him a friendly, open, honest, inviting wink.

EXT. FRED SEGAL'S CLOTHING STORE—DUSK
HARRIS is exiting carrying his goods and an armload of clothes for TRUDI. As he opens the car door for TRUDI, who waits curbside for him to do it, he stops and we see a slow-motion replay of SANDEE and her wink, with an exaggerated crashing sound as the eyelid closes.

EXT. FREEWAY—NIGHT
HARRIS and TRUDI drive along an empty freeway. There is an icy silence in the car. We hear the cough of the engine as it dies out. We hear HARRIS mutter a "shit." The car pulls off the road and into the safety lane, right in front of the digital freeway condition sign, which reads, "FREEWAY CLEAR." HARRIS gets out and raises the hood. TRUDI stays in the car. He fiddles with the engine for a second. A wind comes up and rustles the foliage, blowing against the sign and making a reedlike sound.

HARRIS (*v.o.*)
There are two events in my life that I consider to be magic, that couldn't be explained scientifically. The first of them was about to happen.

He casually looks up at the freeway sign. It reads:

FREEWAY SIGN (*written*)
HIYA.

He does a doubletake and looks around, and goes back to his work. A bulb pops.

                    FREEWAY SIGN (*readout*)
I SAID HIYA.

                              HARRIS
Hi.

                    FREEWAY SIGN (*readout*)
RUOK?

                              HARRIS
RUE-AWK?

                    FREEWAY SIGN (*readout*)
DON'T MAKE ME WASTE LETTERS
R.U.O.K?

                              HARRIS
Oh. Are you okay? Yeah. I'm fine.

                    FREEWAY SIGN (*readout*)
HUG ME.

                              HARRIS
What? Who are you?

                    FREEWAY SIGN (*readout*)
I'M A SIGNPOST.

                              HARRIS
I can see that.

                    FREEWAY SIGN (*readout*)
U CAN'T C MUCH OF ANYTHING. HUG ME.

TRUDI, in the car, hums obliviously.

HARRIS

Wait a minute. I can't just hug you, I've got to get
to know you. (*Under his breath*.) I'm being filmed.
I know I'm being filmed.

FREEWAY SIGN (*readout*)

PLEASE.

HARRIS

All right.

HARRIS looks around, then walks over to the base of the sign and
puts his arms around it. TRUDI, in the car fixing her makeup, is
dead to the world.

FREEWAY SIGN (*readout*)

THAT FELT GOOD.

HARRIS

Is this a joke or something?

FREEWAY SIGN (*readout*)

I C PEOPLE N TROUBLE & I STOP THEM. L.A.
WANTS 2 HELP U.

HARRIS

How am I in trouble?

The car miraculously starts up.

FREEWAY SIGN (*readout*)

U WILL KNOW WHAT 2 DO WHEN U UN-
SCRAMBLE HOW DADDY IS DOING.

HARRIS

What?

IT'S A RIDDLE. U WILL KNOW WHAT 2 DO WHEN
U UNSCRAMBLE HOW DADDY IS DOING.

HARRIS

I'll work on it. 'Bye.

He heads back to the car.

HARRIS *(to Trudi)*

The sign spoke to me.

TRUDI

Uh huh.

HARRIS

It said I was in trouble.

TRUDI

If you're talking to a sign, you are in trouble.

EXT. HARRIS'S APARTMENT—NIGHT
HARRIS and TRUDI pull up; he gets out and tiredly opens the car
door for her so she can get out and then opens the driver's side
door so she can get in to drive home.

HARRIS

I'll see you Sunday?

TRUDI

I've got a shower Sunday.

HARRIS

Oh yeah, and I should really have a bath. How
about Monday?

TRUDI

8:30. You'll pick me up?

HARRIS

8:30? Doesn't anyone eat at six anymore?

A dog starts barking loudly from harris's apartment as he punches in a long code on a keyless electrolock. He opens the fancy beveled-glass wooden door, enters, and we hear the sound of the dog winding down because it's a tape recording.

HARRIS

Good boy.

HARRIS IN HIS APARTMENT

He pushes his cat off a comfy chair and picks enormous amounts of cat hair out of the cushion.

HARRIS (*to cat*)

We could make another cat out of what you leave in this chair.

EXT. SUNRISE—DAY

The sun rises through the smog.

INT. HARRIS'S BEDROOM—DAY

He wakes, groggy, and although the phone is not ringing, he answers it out of habit. The bed is a disaster area of rumpled pillows and blankets.

INT. SARA'S APARTMENT—DAY

SARA wakes. The side of the bed where she has not slept is completely undisturbed.

INT. HARRIS'S BATHROOM—DAY

HARRIS showers.

INT. SARA'S APARTMENT—DAY
SARA showers in slo-mo.

INT. HARRIS'S APARTMENT—DAY
HARRIS sets his shower setting to slo-mo so he can shower slowly too.

INT. SARA'S APARTMENT—DAY
She combs her wet hair.

INT. HARRIS'S APARTMENT—DAY
HARRIS watches an endless stream of junk mail pouring through his mail slot as he stands and eats breakfast. He kicks a trash can in front of the pouring mail.

SARA IN HER APARTMENT
Soundlessly, she sits on the veranda and plays the tuba.

HARRIS IN HIS APARTMENT
His TV is on in the background. He is talking to an electronic telephone, training it to recognize his voice.

                    HARRIS
    Mom . . .

                PHONE (*electronic voice*)
    Mom . . .

                    HARRIS
    Mom . . .

                    PHONE
    Mom . . .

INT. SARA'S APARTMENT—DAY
The TV is on and she watches HARRIS as she tosses a dart at a board. It veers off four feet to the left.

HARRIS (*on the TV*)

(*On video.*) . . . and when the temperature
dropped to 58 this weekend, how did you cope?

MAN

(*On video.*) We just made sure all the windows
were shut.

HARRIS (*on the TV*)

And how about your pets? Were they outside?

She stops throwing the darts, which are everywhere but where
they should be, and watches. Is this for real?

MAN

(*On video.*) The cats were out until around ten but
it got a little too cold for them and they came in.

HARRIS (*on the TV*)

(*Into camera.*) Wow! The cats were out until
around ten but it got a little too cold for them and
they came in. That's how L.A. coped with that
surprise low Saturday night of 58. This is Harris
Telemacher, with the wiggy weekend weather.

SARA jots down a couple of notes.

HARRIS IN HIS APARTMENT

The line starts ringing. He grabs the telephone's instruction book
and starts reading it. Finally he answers it.

HARRIS

Hello, this is Harris. I'm in right now so you can
talk to me personally. Please start talking at the
sound of the beep. Beep.

SARA

Hello, is that Harris Telemacher? This is Sara
McDowel. Do you remember me?

HARRIS

Uh. Yeah. You're the reporter.

SARA

Uh . . . journalist. Yes. And you're the weatherman.

HARRIS

Meteorologist, yeah.

SARA

I hope you don't mind me calling. I just got your
number from Trudi Cowles and I just saw you on
TV and I would love to interview you for my
piece . . .

HARRIS

English, French, or Italian?

SARA

Oh . . . you speak all those languages?

HARRIS

No, if it were Italian or French, I'd be out of it.

Close-up of a dart. She picks up the dart and aims with full con-
centration at a board across the room. Again, it lands in the wall
about four feet to the left.

INT. HARRIS'S APARTMENT—DAY

Still fooling with this voice dialer.

37

                    HARRIS
Mom . . .

                    PHONE (*electronic voice*)
Mom . . .

                    HARRIS
Mom . . .

                    PHONE
Mom . . .

                    HARRIS (*loud*)
Okay, here we go. CALL MOM.

The phone responds by dialing. We hear a voice answer over the speakerphone.

                    VOICE
Domino's Pizza.

                    HARRIS (*shouting*)
Sorry . . . wrong number . . .

EXT. HARRIS'S APARTMENT—DAY
HARRIS's Honda is parked out front. He gets in, drives down three houses, gets out, and bounces up the stairs to another apartment.

INT. ARIEL'S APARTMENT—DAY
ARIEL, thirty-five and attractive. She lives with June, her twenty-eight-year-old roommate. She is sharp, self-reliant, irrepressibly cheerful, and pretty.

                    ARIEL
Want some trail mix? Potato chips? Some cookies?

HARRIS

Ariel, how do you stay thin with all this crap you
have around here?

ARIEL

I guess women burn fat faster than men.

HARRIS

What a romantic notion: Yeah, that's my wife,
pretty, smart, and quite a little fat burner.

ARIEL

You're jealous.

HARRIS

No, I could never be a woman because I'd stay
home all day and play with my breasts.

HARRIS takes out an electronic notepad and marks something down
as he mumbles "true."

ARIEL

What's that for?

HARRIS

I'm writing an article for the Ph.D. Failures News-
letter.

ARIEL

That thing still going?

HARRIS

I'm their lead writer. Where's June?

ARIEL

In her room recovering from the aftereffects of alcohol. Want some juice?

HARRIS

Yeah.

ARIEL

You can be my taster. It's a new mixture for the store.

She hands him a glass of juice. Phone. ARIEL answers it. HARRIS tastes the concoction. Morbid stuff.

HARRIS

It's exactly like licking a shag carpet.

ARIEL

This is Ariel. . . . Hey, kiddo, what's up? . . . This sounds like a job for Supergirl. Okay, I'll come down in about an hour. (*Hangs up.*) It's great being the boss. Can we take your car so I can leave mine for June?

HARRIS

Sure.

JUNE staggers out of the bedroom in her robe, hung over.

ARIEL (*to June*)

Boy, are you gonna have a rough day. There's some coffee and juice in there.

JUNE

Hi, Harris. God, was I stupid.

ARIEL (*concerned*)
I'm gonna make you some eggs. Can you hang on
a minute, Harris?

HARRIS
Sure.

INT. L.A. COUNTY MUSEUM OF ART—SUNDAY
HARRIS and ARIEL look at paintings. ARIEL holds a small home
video camera. They both are looking around sneakily. They
separate. ARIEL goes to one end of a long promenade, filled
with great works of art. HARRIS watches the guard from the
corner of his eye. The guard disappears momentarily around
the corner. HARRIS reaches down and pulls a lever on his shoes.
Roller-skate wheels pop out and he skates the long hallway
while ARIEL videotapes him.

EXT. L.A. COUNTY MUSEUM—DAY
They exit the museum, stifling laughter.

EXT. HARRIS'S APARTMENT—DAY
As HARRIS gets out of his car, SARA arrives, parking on the wrong
side of the street and head to head with HARRIS. She has a camera
and tape recorder in tow.

HARRIS
You're exactly on time.

SARA
I gather being on time is not an L.A. feature.

She starts snapping snaps.

HARRIS
It's one of my features.

41

SARA (*playful*)
I admire that in a man.

HARRIS
If only I were a man it would work out perfectly.

She takes a picture as he stumbles.

HARRIS
Don't use that. Will I be in the *London Times*?

SARA
If you shoot the president maybe. This is for my reference.

HARRIS
I had this idea. Look, rather than do an interview with me, which would be fascinating, by the way, because of my interesting word usements I structure, what if I showed you around town a little? A few secret places.

SARA (*checks her watch*)
Sounds all right.

HARRIS
It's kind of a cultural tour of L.A.

SARA
That's the first fifteen minutes. Then what?

HARRIS
All right, all right. Our first stop's about six blocks from here. Your car or mine?

SARA
Let's walk.

HARRIS
Walk? (*Laughs.*) A walk in L.A.! That's great.
Those crazy English.

SARA (*offended more than she should be*)
What do you mean, crazy? I didn't do anything
crazy, did I?

HARRIS
Yes, you said walk. I said it's about six blocks.
That could mean seven, it could mean eight.

A sweet stare from her. She taps her foot playfully.

HARRIS (*continuing*)
God. You're serious. Okay. Let's go.

EXT. BEVERLY HILLS—DAY

HARRIS
Architecture . . . some of these buildings are over
twenty years old.

Rapid shots of different types of houses. HARRIS comments on their
style with SARA joining in: "French neo-geo Tudor," "English gothic
with perennial Christmas lights" (to be determined by the houses
we actually shoot). One building bears a sign: "This building
available for montage shots."

INT. MUSEUM OF NATURAL HISTORY—DAY

HARRIS (*v.o.*)
Music . . .

The camera pans across an antique cabinet. A sign reads, "VERDI'S BATON," and we see a baton. Then, "MOZART'S QUILL," and we see a quill. Next is a jar on a shelf with something floating in formaldehyde. We take a close look at the label. It says, "BEETHOVEN'S BALLS."

SARA (*v.o.*)
Funny, I thought Margaret Thatcher had them.

EXT. CEMETERY—DAY

HARRIS
Literature . . . not a lot of people are aware of this. . . .

HARRIS and SARA stand in front of a gravestone. HARRIS brushes away some dirt so we can read the marker. "William Shakespeare, born 1564, died 1616. Lived in Los Angeles 1612–14."

HARRIS
I think he wrote "King Henry, Part 8, the Revenge" here.

Nearby a man operates a mechanical grave-digging machine. They're fascinated, and walk over to him. The man gets off the machine and steps into the grave, shoveling debris.

HARRIS
Whose grave is this?

GRAVE DIGGER (*English accent*)
Mine.

SARA
I think he means who's going to be buried here? What's his name?

GRAVE DIGGER

He's not a he, Miss.

HARRIS

All right, all right, she.

GRAVE DIGGER

Not a woman either.

They look at each other, confused.

GRAVE DIGGER (*continuing*)

Used to be a woman. Now she's dead. Ha ha ha.

HARRIS (*to Sara*)

Finally, a funny grave digger.

GRAVE DIGGER

Wanna know how long it takes for a body to rot?

HARRIS

Do we!

GRAVE DIGGER

Well, if they're not already rotten before they die,
eight or nine years. One o' them Beverly Hills
women will last you nine years.

SARA

How come?

GRAVE DIGGER

They've been tan for so many years, their skin
keeps out the water longer and water is something
that can really destroy a very nice dead body.

He brings up a skull out of the grave.

GRAVE DIGGER

Now here's somebody who's been around here
for thirty-five years or more.

HARRIS

Who was that?

GRAVE DIGGER

That there's a magician, name was ... the great
... Blunderman. Not so great now, is he?

HARRIS

The great Blunderman? I knew him, Sara! (*Picks
up the skull.*) God. He was a funny guy. ... He
taught me magic.

SARA (*suddenly quoting*)

... a fellow of infinite jest ...

HARRIS

Yeah ...

SARA

... he hath borne me on his back a thousand
times. ... Where be your gibes now? Your flashes
of merriment, that would set the table on a roar?

HARRIS looks at her.

HARRIS

Ordinarily I don't like to be around interesting
people because it means I have to be interesting,
too.

SARA

Are you saying I'm interesting?

HARRIS

All I know is I find myself trying to show off, which is the idiot's version of being interesting. Are you seeing anyone?

SARA

Uh. Yes.

HARRIS

Me too. So that's sort of out.

SARA

I suppose it is.

HARRIS

It would be wrong, wouldn't it?

SARA

If we were to start a relationship, that would be the wrong way to start it.

HARRIS

Yes, it would.

SARA

Especially since you live here and I live there.

HARRIS

Too difficult.

GRAVE DIGGER

Could you give your friend's head back?

HARRIS

I should get to work.

SARA

Well, let's not just stand here like a couple of nits.
Let's go.

INT. HARRIS'S APARTMENT—DAY

He's throwing on his tie and coat. He goes over and turns
the art calendar page from a Mondrian to a Rousseau jungle
painting. Then, he picks up little rain and sun symbols that
he uses on the TV show and places them strategically on the
Rousseau.

INT. TV STUDIO—DAY

The floor director cues HARRIS and he starts the weather report in
the studio.

HARRIS

What a weekend! We've got sun, earth, and atmo-
sphere, and when you got that, you've got weather!
Good weather. Anyone with half a brain will be out
this weekend, which is exactly what most of you
have, because it's going to be fabulous. Lots and
lots of sun. Here's the financial report: 89 Mercedes
up four hundred dollars at $28,640, used 88
Mercedes unchanged at $23,100.

A moment goes by.

HARRIS

And cut.

We see the studio and cameramen.

HARRIS

So you'll run that for me on Saturday, okay, Jesse?

JESSE
Should you really be pretaping the weather report?

HARRIS
The weekends are very tough for me to come in.
You can imagine my busy weekend schedule.
Besides, this is L.A. What's going to change?

EXT. MELROSE—DAY
It's six o'clock on Sunday. It's raining. HARRIS looks out of his car,
dismayed, at the thunderheads. He passes Fred Segal's and remembers his pants. He pulls in.

HARRIS (*v.o.*)
There are two reasons for the ridiculous detour I
was about to embark on. The first reason was I
believed a relationship with Sara was impossible.
And the second reason was, I was a big dumb
male.

EXT. FRED SEGAL'S PARKING LOT—DAY
The store has just closed. He walks up to the door just as SANDEE
is leaving. She passes him on the sidewalk.

HARRIS
Closed?

SANDEE
Yeah, sorry.

She continues on past and he watches her. After a moment of
decision, he says:

HARRIS
I just came to pick up my pants.

                        SANDEE
Yeah?

                        HARRIS
You sold me a pair of pants and a tie thing.

                        SANDEE
Oh yeah, I remember. You just want to pick them
up?

                        HARRIS
Yeah.

                        SANDEE
I can get them for you.

                        HARRIS
That would be great. It would save me coming
back.

                        SANDEE
It wouldn't be so bad if you had to come back.

She walks back and raps on the door for them to let her in.

                        HARRIS
I don't have my ticket.

                        SANDEE
That's okay. I remember what they look like. God,
I'm getting all wet.

The door is opened for her. HARRIS waits. Momentarily she reappears, empty-handed. She still hangs in the door.

SANDEE (*continuing*)

They're not ready. You want us to call you when
they are?

HARRIS

Oh. Okay.

She gets a Fred Segal business card.

SANDEE

What's the number?

They walk away from the door a few feet.

HARRIS

Here, I'll write it . . . there.

He hands her the card; she pockets it.

SANDEE

Okay, I'll have them call you. It'll probably be
tomorrow. 'Bye.

She gives him that slo-mo wink again. HARRIS watches her walk
off again.

EXT. SANTA MONICA FREEWAY—NIGHT

HARRIS drives along, nearing the digital freeway traffic sign. Right
in the middle of the flashing messages, SAVE GAS, CARPOOL—
TRAFFIC CLEAR AHEAD, etc., flashes the message:

FREEWAY SIGN

U SHOULD HAVE GOT HER NUMBER.

INT. HARRIS'S APARTMENT—NIGHT

HARRIS, glass of wine in hand, is writing with paint in reverse on his window, "Bored Beyond Belief." The phone rings. He turns and looks at the phone.

INT. HARD ROCK CAFE—CLOSE-UP—SANDEE—NIGHT

We can see the action behind her and hear the music throbbing noisily. The joint is jumping. They are drinking, HARRIS a little high.

                    SANDEE
Were you shocked?

                    HARRIS
Shocked but glad.

                    SANDEE
I could tell you wanted to ask me for my number
so I just asked for yours.

                    HARRIS
But I didn't know I wanted to ask for your number
till it was too late.

                    SANDEE
I went to this psychic once. I don't really believe in
that stuff, but he told me I had a special fifth sense
about things.

                    HARRIS
You mean about guys wanting your number? I
think you could probably just figure everyone.

                    SANDEE
Oh, that's sweet.

HARRIS

God, I can't help but be nervous out here.

SANDEE

You're not really doing anything wrong.

HARRIS

Ha. I am doing something so wrong you can't
believe it. This is worthy of the death penalty. Jeez,
you must have a boyfriend . . .

SANDEE

He doesn't care. He can't care. He gave me this
big speech about how he wanted his freedom.
Even though we live together, he still wanted to
go out. So, I said okay, but it backfires on him
every once in awhile.

HARRIS

Where is he now?

SANDEE

He's over at the bar.

HARRIS

What?!

They look over at the bar. Indeed there is a very nervous boyfriend, sort of wimpy looking, standing at the bar with a beer
and trying not to look at them.

SANDEE

Don't worry, this is his idea. You want my number?

53

HARRIS

No! That would be a disaster. No, I don't want the
number. If I had the number I might call you.

SANDEE

It's 555-2312. Say it back.

HARRIS

I can't. No.

SANDEE

555-2312. Say it back.

HARRIS

No.

SANDEE (*slowly and deliberate*)

Five. Five. Five. Two. Three. One. Two.

HARRIS

No! God, you're going to make me memorize it.

SANDEE (*again*)

Five. Five. Five. Two. Three. One. Two.

HARRIS

Damn it! Now I know it. 555-2312. (*Continuing.*)
Would you tell me your name again?

SANDEE

SanDee.

HARRIS

I like that name. Everybody has weird names now.
Tiffany spelled with a "ph" or, instead of Nancy, it's
Nanceen.

> SANDEE (*spells it for him*)

Big S . . . small a . . . small n . . . big d, small e,
big e.

> HARRIS

What?

She takes out a pen and writes it down for him.

> SANDEE

Big S . . . small a . . . small n . . . big d, small e, big
e. SanDeE. And there's a star at the end.

We see the signature in extreme close-up.

EXT. HARD ROCK CAFE—NIGHT

SANDEE and nervous HARRIS exit. They walk out of frame, and in
the distance, walking toward the entrance, we see TRUDI and FRANK,
arm in arm.

EXT. TAIL O' THE PUP—NIGHT

HARRIS and SANDEE get in line at an automated night teller, waiting
in line behind three others. We now see there is another line at
the night teller, that of criminals. As each person gets his money,
the next crook in line pulls a gun and takes it from them. The
whole thing is very polite.

> SANDEE

When I got out of class, I decided to call you.

> HARRIS

What class are you taking?

> SANDEE

I'm studying to be a spokesmodel.

HARRIS

What's a spokesmodel?

SANDEE

You know, a model who speaks . . . points at
things like merchandise.

He is now at the front of the line. He gets the money, and almost immediately, the next CROOK in line walks over to them.

CROOK

Hi, my name is Bob and I'll be your robber.

He hands the money over as if it were all in a typical L.A. day.
They get in the car and as his car pulls out, it passes ROLAND
DRAKE and SARA, who stand talking in front of the Tail o' the
Pup eating dogs as a roller skater glides by.

EXT. TAIL O' THE PUP—NIGHT
ROLAND and SARA milling.

ROLAND

So why won't you sleep with me?

SARA

People don't sleep with their ex-husbands.

ROLAND

It happens all the time. Who knows, it might be
just like it was.

SARA

Oh Roland, that would be terrible.

ROLAND

Come on, Sara. We're a perfect match.

SARA

Just because your mother hunts with my mother doesn't make us a perfect match.

ROLAND

That's not what I'm saying, for God's sake. Your mother shot my mother with a . . .

SARA

That was an accident. And it was only in the foot.

ROLAND

You're the normal one in the family and you're just barely hanging on. Remember when your mother found out whose dog it was that kept crapping in front of your house and she wrote their name on a little flag and stuck it into the center of the pile?

SARA

Oh God. They skewered me at school for that. . . .

ROLAND

And when your father appeared on the BBC news because he peeled a lemon rind into an unbroken twenty-four-foot strip?

SARA

It was only twenty-two feet.

ROLAND

I remember you crying for a week. These are not things grown-ups do. I'm the only sane thing in your life.

SARA

It's true. I want a quiet life.

ROLAND

I want you back. All I'm asking for is one weekend with you. We'll go away and see how it is.

A roller skater glides silently by.

SARA

I went roller-skating once at the Brooklyn Roller-drome. I got completely out of control . . . I couldn't turn and I couldn't stop. And I ran into this black guy, eight feet tall, emerald-green satin jumpsuit, matching skates—very stoned—and I said, "I'm really sorry, perhaps you could help me." And he looked down at me and he said, "Little lady, let your mind go and your body will follow."

ROLAND takes her and kisses her. A long one. It's almost passion-ate. Her eyes open during the kiss. They break.

ROLAND

Well, how was that?

SARA

I give it a five.

EXT. SANDEE'S HOUSE—NIGHT
HARRIS drops SANDEE off at her place.

HARRIS

Well, I hope I wasn't too young in my thinking for you.

SANDEE

What?

HARRIS

Joke.

SANDEE

I didn't put any pressure on you, did I?

HARRIS

Not at all. I don't pressure you, do I?

SANDEE

No. I don't think there should be pressure.

HARRIS

Tell me if I pressure you.

SANDEE

Okay. You too. But don't feel like you have to.
Have you ever had a high colonic?

HARRIS

Pardon me?

SANDEE

A high colonic.

HARRIS

You mean an enema?

SANDEE

Yeah.

HARRIS

I keep waiting for you to say "joke."

SANDEE

They're great. They really purify you. There's a
place in Santa Monica run by Vishnus that do it.

HARRIS

Well, g'night.

SANDEE

G'night.

She takes steps up to him and gives him a teen-age open-
mouthed kiss. HARRIS retreats to his car.

INT. HARRIS'S APARTMENT—DAY

The phone rings. HARRIS answers with the speakerphone.

HARRIS

Hello?

TRUDI

Take me off the goddamn speakerphone!

HARRIS

Relax. It's just a modern-day device.

TRUDI

I have to see you.

INT. TRUDI'S APARTMENT—DAY

TRUDI is anxious.

HARRIS

You were with someone else last night?

TRUDI

Yes.

HARRIS

There was no shower?

TRUDI

There was. I didn't go at the last minute.

HARRIS *(joking)*

Having sex with my agent again. I've told you a
thousand times . . .

She looks up, shocked.

TRUDI

How did you know?

HARRIS

I was right? I was right? I was making a bad joke.
My agent? Frank? And this is how I find out . . . you
tell me?

TRUDI

He's not happy about it either. We just decided
that I should tell you.

HARRIS

God, I thought he was only supposed to take ten
percent.

TRUDI

We were here, and then afterwards . . .

HARRIS

Oh, God, afterwards . . . yes, after he made love
to you . . . what?

61

TRUDI

We went out to the Hard Rock Cafe . . .

HARRIS (*whoops*)

What time?

TRUDI

Oh, I don't know, 11:00, 11:30. But I felt I had to tell you in case anyone saw us there. It was a real dumb thing to do.

HARRIS

How long has this been going on?

TRUDI

Three years. I'm sorry.

HARRIS

Three years? This has been going on since the eighties? I don't think I can be here right now.

He looks torn up. He backs out of the house.

EXT. TRUDI'S—DAY

He comes out the front door. On his back, we see a man shaken, sad, forlorn. He walks about twenty-five feet and the walk becomes one of great elation.

EXT. SANTA MONICA FREEWAY—NIGHT

HARRIS speaks to the sign.

HARRIS

Yes! Yes! Yes! L.A., I love ya! I'm out of the relationship, I'm out of my agency, and I only had to look like a sucker for three years! . . . and I come

off like the good guy. I got what I want, and
nobody can blame me! You really did it. Thanks,
L.A.

FREEWAY SIGN (*readout*)
U SHOULD B THANKFUL 4 THE WEATHER.

HARRIS
What do you mean?

FREEWAY SIGN (*readout*)
THE WEATHER WILL CHANGE YOUR LIFE.
TWICE.

HARRIS (*irritated*)
Who are you? The Oracle at Delphi?

FREEWAY SIGN (*readout*)
READ MY LIGHTS. THE WEATHER WILL
CHANGE YOUR LIFE.

HARRIS
Have you always been a signpost? I mean, did
you start out as a stop sign then become a
streetlight and then a billboard . . .

FREEWAY SIGN (*readout*)
I BELIEVE I WAS REINCARNATED FROM A
BAGPIPE. LISTEN.

It puffs an out-of-tune low moan.

FREEWAY SIGN (*readout*)
O 2 HAVE MY VOICE BACK.

HARRIS

You and me both. Well, bye. Try not to wander off too far. (*Laughs at his own joke.*) Sorry, I couldn't resist.

He walks away; a bulb pops.

FREEWAY SIGN (*readout*)

HARRIS, WOULD U DO ME A FAVOR?

HARRIS

Sure.

FREEWAY SIGN (*readout*)

THERE'S A SIGN ON THE VENTURA FREEWAY.
WE TALK SOMETIMES ON THE UNDERGROUND. I
LIKE HER. COULD U TAKE A LOOK 4 ME?

HARRIS nods yes. He leaves.

INT. TV STUDIO—DAY

HARRIS is arguing with the same head of the news operation, TOD.

HARRIS

. . . Oh so now it's not about the gags; it's about the weather.

TOD

It was always about the weather.

During HARRIS's next two speeches, TOD keeps muttering to his female assistant, who is dressed like an MTV host, "Tell Gail we need more chatter as the credits roll and it would be great if it looked like she and Jerry were falling in love."

HARRIS

No, no, no. It was never about the weather. It was
always about the gags. If you wanted someone
who could predict the weather, you would have
hired a meteorologist. I distinctly remember you
saying you wanted to make the weather not so
much of a tune-out.

TOD

Yes, but along with that you had to have a fairly
accurate forecast.

HARRIS

Hey, so some weekend sailors lost some boats. Big
deal. If they were rich enough to have a boat, they
were rich enough to lose it. And what kind of an
asshole sailor would trust the wacky weekend
weatherman, anyway?

TOD has entered the elevator.

TOD

This one. You're fired.

The doors should have closed on the line, but they didn't.

TOD

I mean it, you're fired.

HARRIS (*muttering to himself*)
That's once.

INT. TV STUDIO—DAY
As HARRIS walks down a hall, MORRIS FROST walks toward him.

MORRIS

Hey Harris, I heard you broke up with Trudi. I
always figured your relationship was a "two."

Without breaking stride, HARRIS clangs MORRIS's head on a fire bell.

EXT. STREET—DAY

HARRIS is leaning out of his car using a pay phone.

HARRIS

Mr. Harry Zell, please. I'm calling from my car. This
is Harris K. Telemacher, the wacky weatherman.
. . . Oh you do? Uh, hang on a minute and let me
get rid of this other call.

He puts his hand over the mouthpiece and waits, then gets back
on.

HARRIS

I'm back.

EXT. OUTDOOR RESTAURANT—DAY

A lively Hollywood outdoor cafe. HARRIS approaches the MAITRE
D', who casts an especially sniveling look at him.

HARRIS

I'm meeting Harry Zell.

MAITRE D' (*suddenly perking up*)

Really? You? How?

HARRIS doesn't answer. Then:

MAITRE D' (*desperate*)

Please . . .

HARRIS

He happens to be a fan of the weekend weather.

MAITRE D'

Mr. Zell's table is right over there.

HARRIS waits. Suddenly from the sky a man flying with a rocket pack hovers over the restaurant and lands at the entrance. He steps briskly out of the contraption. It is HARRY ZELL. He is everything you would like to be: good-looking, Wasp, early forties, not neurotic, well-groomed. He rushes over to his table. The waiter immediately sets down Zell's usual order and he begins eating. Simultaneously, HARRIS is brought a cheaper, smaller version of the same thing.

HARRY ZELL

I've scheduled an interview here for after I've finished eating? Do you mind?

HARRIS

No, no, not at all. I'll just slither out.

HARRY ZELL

First, let me say I took this meeting because my kids really enjoy your work. That impresses me.

HARRIS

Thank you. I try to make it interes . . .

HARRY ZELL

Three ideas in town I'd like to try you on. One: a comedy. Dark night, girl gets raped two months before her wedding night.

HARRIS

Did you say comedy?

HARRY ZELL

She gets married, but then she realizes she's
pregnant. Big hubbub. Husband, mad, etc. Happy
ending: she finds out it was the husband who
raped her.

A weak, sniveling "that's a great idea" laugh from HARRIS.

HARRY ZELL

That could be very big. Here's another, my own
idea: A department store Santa gets his suit stolen
on Christmas eve . . . we find out later he's the real
Santa . . . that's a holiday idea. . . . Think about it.
You can write it. If you don't want to write it, you
can be in it. If you don't want to be in it, you can
direct it. Two: I'm thinking of opening a Broadway musical over on Melrose. It's like "La Cage aux
Folles," only prostitutes. First act closing song is . . .
spotlight up on a lone girl center stage. She sings,
(*singing*) I FUCK FOR A LIV——ING! Another
spotlight up, another prostitute: I DO TOO!

Everyone in the restaurant looks around.

HARRY ZELL (*continuing*)

You could be in it. I skimmed some of your writing, by the way. Also, *The Enquirer* and *People* are
going to do personal attacks on Scot Johns next
week so they may not want him for the "Dad is
Love" miniseries.

HARRIS

Why are they going to do personal attacks on him?

HARRY ZELL

Just part of the "new cruelty." The first thing I'd like to do is send you out on some commercial auditions.

HARRIS

Great!

HARRY ZELL

I'm going to work on the Hollywood Day Parade for you but I don't know.

HARRY has finished eating. The WAITER comes over.

WAITER

Your interview is here, Mr. Zell.

HARRY ZELL

Perfect, I'm just finished.

HARRIS gets up, knowing his lunch is over.

HARRIS

Mr. Zell, how was I? In the meeting.

ZELL (*taking his hand and looking him straight in the eye*)
You were good.

HARRIS

Any advice?

HARRY ZELL

Sure . . . skipping. (*Leaning in.*) Skipping is a perfect compromise between running and walking. It looks too desperate if you run to a meeting.

HARRIS

I'll remember that.

SARA appears with her notepad in hand. She is Zell's interview.
HARRIS sees her. He nods hello.

HARRIS

You're all over town, I see.

SARA

You too. I'm meeting Harry Zell.

HARRIS

I just spent an hour with him . . . (*checks his
watch*) uh, no, ten minutes.

A MAN approaches HARRIS.

MAN

How are you?

HARRIS (*excited*)

Hey, how are you? What's going on?

MAN

The usual . . . we've got a terrific project develop-
ing. Should be fabulous. . . .

HARRIS

Sounds exciting . . .

MAN

Well, we'll see. I think it's going to be great.

HARRIS

That *really* sounds exciting.

70

MAN

I'll give you a call.

The MAN exits. HARRIS waits till he's completely gone. The wind
blows sara's napkin on the ground. They bend to pick it up.

SARA

Who was that?

HARRIS

Not a clue. By the way, I need to talk to you . . .
something's changed and . . .

The MAN reappears next to HARRIS.

MAN

Hey, we're having cocktails tonight around six.
Why don't you two stop by?

HARRIS

You remember Eloise . . .

MAN

Oh, yes! How are you? You're looking fantastic.

SARA

Fine. I so admire your work.

MAN

Oh, well thanks!

HARRIS (*to Sara*)

What do you think, honey? Sounds great . . . same
address?

MAN

The very same. See you there.

HARRIS
Oh, thanks. (*To Sara, making a "v" sign with his fingers.*) He and I are like this. Are you still seeing someone? Because . . .

HARRY ZELL raps loudly on the table. HARRIS departs, frustrated.

EXT. HARRIS'S APARTMENT—NIGHT
He gets in his car and drives the three doors to Ariel's apartment.

INT. ARIEL'S APARTMENT—NIGHT
We see a close-up of a TV screen. On it are various shots of HARRIS roller-skating at the LACMA. Being typed on the screen via ariel's editing equipment are the words, "Harris K. Telemacher's World of Art." ARIEL and HARRIS talk as they edit the tape.

HARRIS (*v.o.*)
When I really analyze it, Trudi wasn't for me anyway. The only good times we had were having sex and laying in bed watching TV.

ARIEL (*v.o.*)
Harris, I hate to tell you this, but if you've got someone you can have great sex with and lie in bed and watch TV, you've really got something.

HARRIS winces. JUNE approaches off-screen.

JUNE (*v.o.*)
Anyone want anything?

HARRIS (*v.o.*)
Yeah, I'll have a nonalcoholic beer.

JUNE (*v.o.*)
(*Mocking him.*) "I'll have a nonalcoholic beer."

72

ARIEL (*v.o.*)

Oh, shut up and go punch some cattle. (*Continuing, to Harris.*) How do you like wading through a sea of estrogen? Anyone else out there on the horizon?

HARRIS (*v.o.*)

(*Thinks.*) No . . . no, not that I can think of.

ARIEL (*v.o.*)

So why don't you call this SanDee girl? At least you'd have someone to take places.

The tape winds forward or backward depending on harris's mood shifts.

HARRIS (*v.o.*)

Yeah, maybe I should. It's someone to be with. . . . Wait, what am I saying? It's the road to nowhere. She's into astrology and spinning around. . . . I mean, she's really nice so it definitely a possibility, maybe I should . . . but . . . no, no, I don't know. . . . I feel like if anybody sees me with her, they'd know I'm with her strictly for sex. It's embarrassing.

ARIEL (*v.o.*)

So let's see. That would make you the first man to see a woman strictly for sex.

HARRIS (*v.o.*)

Yeah, I don't want to go down in the history books as the first man to see a woman only for sex. Other men would make fun of me. . . .

ARIEL (*v.o.*)
Do you think she would care?

HARRIS (*v.o.*)
No . . . she probably wouldn't, maybe I should . . .
(*Thinks a moment.*) Wait, what am I saying? No,
no, I'm not going to call her. I'll call her just to talk.

EXT. STREET—NIGHT

EXT. STREET—DAY
SANDEE and HARRIS (wearing the new tie he bought at Fred Segal's)
exit the Vishnu high-colonic center. HARRIS is walking a little funny.

SANDEE
Well, whad'ya think?

HARRIS
I think it was a total washout.

SANDEE (*as they walk*)
It really clears out your head.

HARRIS
Head? Boy, you should run back in there and tell
them they're doing it wrong. Well, it was a great
lunch and enema. (*Then.*) How about Friday? You
available Friday?

SANDEE
Sure. Hey, I heard of a new restaurant that's supposed to be great. On Sunset . . . uh . . . L'Idiot?

*As they walk out of shot, the camera pans up to see the Vishnu
logo of a face with pointed horns and a tongue sticking out of its
mouth and pointing up in the air.*

74

INT. HARRIS'S APARTMENT—DAY

HARRIS picks up the phone and dials L'Idiot.

HARRIS

Hi, L'Idiot? I'd like to make reservations for two for
Friday . . .

A faint sound of laughter coming through the phone.

HARRIS

How about Saturday? . . . Sunday? . . . Okay,
good . . . 8:30. 5:30 or 10:30? 5:30. What? I'm a
weatherman, why? I've done plays and some
commercials . . . renting. Well, I don't see how
that's any business of yours. In the low fifties. . . .
Well, I just sold a condo. Yes, Visa. And
MasterCard. All right, I guess I could meet you
there at three.

EXT. PARKING LOT—DAY

A car speeds into the parking space. A tardy HARRIS gets out of
his car and skips out of the covered parking lot and across the
street to the Fourth Reich Bank of Hamburg. People eye him
curiously.

INT. BANK—DAY

HARRIS sits at bank exec's desk across from snobby FRENCH RESTAU-
RANTEUR. A CHEF stands in the background and is constantly
checked with by the FRENCHMAN. harris's files are spread out on
the desk.

HARRIS

I have Visa, MasterCard . . .

FRENCHMAN (*with disgust*)

They all have Visa and MasterCard.

EXEC

I think what Mr. Pardeau is looking for is more than a promise to pay. He's looking for a kind of depth in your financial sea, so to speak.

FRENCHMAN

Let's make this easier. Suppose you get the reservation and let's suppose you come down to the restaurant and we honor it. What do you think you might order?

He produces one of the huge, unmanageable menus. HARRIS examines it.

HARRIS

Well, I might like to have the duck. . . .

CHEF

He can't have the duck.

FRENCHMAN

You can't have the duck.

HARRIS

Why?

FRENCHMAN (*barely controlling his anger*)
You think with a financial statement like this you can have the duck?! Where do you summer?

HARRIS

What do you mean?

FRENCHMAN

Where do you summer?

                              HARRIS
     Right here.

The CHEF smirks at this.

                               CHEF
     He can have the chicken.

                            FRENCHMAN
     You can have the chicken.

                              HARRIS
     Chicken only?

                            FRENCHMAN
     You can have a salad and the chicken and a piece
     of bread.

                              HARRIS
     What about my date? I can't tell her what to order.

                            FRENCHMAN
     You can certainly urge her in one direction.

                              HARRIS
     Look, either we go there and she orders what she
     wants or forget it.

The FRENCHMAN sweats a little and goes over the financial statement with a calculator. Finally:

                            FRENCHMAN
     All right. I like a little gamble. We can take you in
     eight weeks.

INT. HARRIS'S APARTMENT—DAY

HARRIS on the phone. During the conversation, TRUDI enters with a key and takes some of her books and picture frames.

> HARRIS
>
> SanDee? Hi. Listen, I've heard some bad things about L'Idiot. I read a review that only gave it four stars. A restaurant like that should have twenty or twenty-five. What if we went away this weekend? How would that be?

The squeal forces Harris's ear away from the phone.

INT. SARA'S APARTMENT—DAY

She speaks into her tape recorder.

> SARA
>
> Some say L.A.'s a place for the brain-dead. . . . Roland says it's a place where if you turned off the sprinklers, it would turn into a desert . . . check that quote . . . but I don't know, it's not what I ex- pected. I say . . . it's a place where they have taken a desert and turned it into their dreams. In fact, it's oddly familiar.

MONTAGE OVER SARA'S MONOLOGUE

ARIEL on a massage table in her backyard being beaten gently with palm leaves by two guys in turbans. JUNE gives herself a pedicure on a wicker outdoor chaise.

SANDEE in a spokesmodel class learning to point at merchandise.

TRUDI in her apartment getting ready to go out while FRANK reads magazines patiently in the background.

HARRY ZELL skipping with several businessmen across a studio lot.

INT. TEMPORARY CONTEMPORARY ART MUSEUM—DAY

SARA and ROLAND tour the museum. SARA talks into her tape recorder. SARA looks very different from her "work" look. She is dressed casually and looks almost girlish.

> SARA (*v.o.*)
> (*Continuous with above.*) I've seen a lot of L.A.,
> and I say it's also a place of secrets. Secret houses,
> secret lives, secret pleasures, and no one is looking
> to the outside for verification that what they're
> doing is all right. What do you say, Roland?

> ROLAND
> I still say it's a place for the brain-dead.

> SARA
> Why do you have to be so snotty? Really, I think
> you're just being superior. I've met some pretty
> intelligent people here in Los Angeles.

In the background HARRIS skates by a museum portal. We see in extra close-up a spot of water on the floor. Suddenly, from nowhere, he smashes into SARA, almost knocking her over. ARIEL comes up, carting the video camera.

> ROLAND
> Am I crazy or were you roller-skating?

> HARRIS
> This is way more important than roller-skating.

> SARA
> Have you tried the Guggenheim?

> HARRIS
> I get that. I really do. It's circular and it goes
> downhill.

ARIEL

Got it. Oh hi.

ROLAND

Could we get deported for this? I can feel my
green card turning brown.

SARA

Harris Telemacher, this is Roland Drake. We all
had lunch together.

HARRIS

This is my friend Ariel Dunne. This is Roland
Drake and Sara . . .

SARA

McDowel.

ARIEL

Hi.

ROLAND

I loved your wacky TV bit.

HARRIS

Thank you, I loved yours too.

ROLAND

But I didn't . . . oh I see . . . marvelously funny.
You have a lot of verve.

HARRIS

Verve?

SARA

Would you like to walk around with us?

HARRIS

Sure.

INT. TEMPORARY CONTEMPORARY ART MUSEUM—DAY

From the painting's point of view we see the four of them
looking at a picture. Behind them is an Italian job with
lots of people getting their heads cut off (or something like
that).

HARRIS

I like the relationships; each character has its
own story. I mean, the puppy is a little too much
but sometimes you have to overlook things like
that. But the way he's holding her! . . . It's almost
filthy. He's about to kiss her, she's pulling away
a little . . . the way his leg is smashed up against
her. And look how nicely he painted her blouse,
kind of loose, transparent; you can see her breast
under it touching him about here. . . . (*He indicates.*) It's pretty torrid. And look at the people
peeking from the doorway all shocked. They
wish. When I see a painting like this, I must
admit, I get a little . . . well let's just say . . .
uh . . . emotionally . . . erect.

We see the painting he's talking about. It's a big ten-by-twenty-
foot canvas that is solid pink.

EXT. TEMPORARY CONTEMPORARY ART MUSEUM—DUSK

The four of them have exited the museum.

ROLAND

Well, that was terrific. All those paintings of food
made me hungry.

HARRIS
Yes, I could eat some paintings of food myself.

They ad-lib good-byes, and the two couples separate. We can see SARA and ROLAND chatting; then SARA turns back.

SARA
Why don't we go somewhere for dinner?

HARRIS
I've heard about this happening, where you meet someone coincidentally and you end up having dinner with them, but it never actually happened to me.

ROLAND finds HARRIS frightfully amusing and laughs aloud.

HARRIS (*continuing; to Ariel, sotto voce*)
This guy loves me.

They approach.

ROLAND
We could stop by L'Idiot.

HARRIS
Great. But I should warn you, we'll never get in L'Idiot; it's impossible.

ROLAND spots a pay phone.

ARIEL
I have to meet June. Could they take you home?

HARRIS
I don't want to impose. . . .

SARA

No problem at all. We've got two cars.

ROLAND

All set.

SARA

You better ride with me since you know where
it is.

HARRIS (*overjustifying*)

Yeah, I know where it is so that would be easier
since Sara probably doesn't know and I could tell
her and you know already.

EXT. STREET—DAY

SARA and HARRIS get in her car. She drives off on the left side of
the street, swerving over at the last minute.

EXT. L'IDIOT PARKING LOT—NIGHT

HARRIS and SARA arrive in their car as photographers' cameras click
at celebrities. When SARA and HARRIS pass them, they see who it
is; they get immediately bored and their cameras fall sicken-
ingly silent. They walk into the restaurant, and we see the sign
of the restaurant, L'IDIOT.

INT. L'IDIOT—NIGHT

Hollywood. It's the "in place," and it is packed with "in people."
The MAITRE D' who interrogated HARRIS at the bank approaches.

MAITRE D'

Yes, Mr. Drake, for three. Right this way.

He takes note of HARRIS suspiciously. As they go to the table, HARRIS
passes FRANK, sitting at a table for two, alone.

83

                        HARRIS
Hi, Frank.

                        FRANK
Oh, hello, Harris. Nice to see you.

                        HARRIS
Trudi here?

                        FRANK
She'll be here any minute. Any problem?

                        HARRIS
No, no; but she'll understand if I don't come over
and say hello.

                        FRANK
Sure.

                        HARRIS
Hey, Frank. One question. When did you and Trudi
find time to get together?

                        FRANK
You won't be mad?

                        HARRIS
No.

                        FRANK
While you were doing the jobs I got you.

HARRIS backs off. They are seated just as ROLAND arrives. HARRIS sits
and stares at FRANK and we see his slight smile of satisfaction at
watching someone else wait for TRUDI.

INT. TABLE—NIGHT
A waiter arrives at the table.

WAITER (*rap style*)
I'm gonna tell you
what we got to eat.
We got two kinds of pasta,
Six different kinds of meat.

We got side cuts, end cuts,
covered with a goo,
called hollandaise, bernaise,
and we can broil it, too.

We got crab cakes, zucchini flakes,
Artichokes and more,
Santa Barbara Oysters on a
bed of grilled raddichio.

We got spicy guacamole and
a Brie quesadilla,
we got goat-cheese pizza on a
blue corn tortilla.

We got hot bread, milk-fed veal
and new potatoes,
and a hundred different ways
to cook a couple of tomatoes.

If the service is a problem
'cause the place is packed,
ask for me, I'm Sam the waiter
and I also act.

Close-up: A tight shot of the tiniest portion of food imaginable being delivered to our group.

85

HARRIS (*looking at the plate*)
Gee, I'm done already and I don't remember eating.

WAITER
Floss?

ROLAND
I'll have some.

WAITER
Diet or regular?

ROLAND
Regular, please.

ROLAND begins flossing. SARA begins an out-of-control giggle. HARRIS joins in.

EXT. L'IDIOT—NIGHT
They exit the restaurant. The flashbulbs fall still again.

EXT. PARKING LOT—NIGHT
They are at the valet lot. ROLAND is busy handing the tickets to the valet. "It's the blue one with the convertible top. . . ." SARA and HARRIS are left alone.

SARA
I'll take you home. I love close to you.

HARRIS
You what?

SARA
I live close to you.

ROLAND rejoins them.

SARA

I'll take him home; he's on the way.

ROLAND

That's perfect since I live in the valley.

Three valet parkers scoff.

HARRIS (*nervous about her driving*)

Maybe I should take a cab.

SARA

Don't be silly.

He gets in and tightly secures his seat belt. The car zooms out of frame. We stay on the empty frame and hear HARRIS shouting, "Right side . . . right side!"

EXT. HARRIS'S APARTMENT—NIGHT
HARRIS bolts out of the car. He has a look of mortal fear.

HARRIS (*eyeing her*)

It was really fun.

SARA (*buoyant*)

Yes, it was.

She goes back to business.

HARRIS (*searching*)

I like Roland a lot.

SARA

He's nice, isn't he.

HARRIS is desperately trying to find out if ROLAND is Sara's beau.

We, and SARA, see the writing in the window behind him, "Bored Beyond Belief." Silence.

HARRIS

Well, good night.

SARA

Good night.

He starts to go inside. Suddenly, silently, Sara's car starts to slowly roll. SARA utters her concern. HARRIS watches for a moment, tries the car door; it's locked. He tries to stop the car by pulling on the bumper; it continues to roll. Then, magically, both car doors unlatch. HARRIS pauses a moment and realizes something is going on.

HARRIS

Get in.

SARA

What?

HARRIS

Get in.

He runs between the car and her while he speaks.

SARA

NO.

HARRIS

I know this looks weird but it's not. This is a completely safe mysteriously rolling car.

SARA

What's going on?

HARRIS

Do you realize "This is a completely safe mysteriously rolling car" is a sentence which probably has never been said in the history of the universe? Please, get in.

She capitulates. They get in the car as it rolls away silently.

EXT. FREEWAY—NIGHT
Sara's car rolls up and stops at the freeway sign. HARRIS gets out of the car and looks up at it. It is blank.

HARRIS (*to the sign*)

What is it?

SARA gets out of the car.

SARA (*slowly*)

I haven't said a thing. I accepted the roller-skating, I accepted the flossing. I even partially accepted the moving car. I like you but it gets harder and harder. I left home to get away from exactly this.

SARA has walked forward and turned her back to the sign. Suddenly, behind Sara's back, the sign lights up!

FREEWAY SIGN (*readout*)

KISS HER, YOU FOOL.

Big animated lips purse on the screen. HARRIS steps forward and kisses her hard. They part, breathless. The sign sputters, as though reading Sara's mind. It glows its next line:

FREEWAY SIGN (*readout*)
LET YOUR MIND GO AND YOUR BODY WILL
FOLLOW.

SARA, her back to the sign, looks up at HARRIS.

SARA
My head hurts.

He kisses her again.

SARA
It's getting late. I should go.

EXT. HARRIS'S APARTMENT—NIGHT
She drops him off. They linger around each other, hovering.

HARRIS
Do you want to come in?

SARA (*not stupid*)
Why?

HARRIS
Yeah, yeah. We're moving too fast. But, you know, we should see each other again.

SARA
I guess, yes, I guess we should.

HARRIS
What's today?

SARA
Thursday.

HARRIS
The weekend?

SARA
I should tell you, I'm supposed to see my ex this
weekend. It's part of the deal.

HARRIS
Oh God, I can't this weekend either. I've got a few
things to untangle myself. My mom throws a bridge
lunch thing that I have to be at. . . . Hey, I've got to
go to some fund-raising dinner tomorrow. You
want to go? Might be interesting for you to see how
boring something can be. Not a date . . . just a do.

SARA
All right. All right. Bye. By the way, I think it's
wonderful that you see your mother. It reminds me
I should call mine.

EXT. HARRIS'S APARTMENT—NIGHT
He walks up to the front door. His front door is gone. He picks
up a note taped to the entrance.

HARRIS
Good grief.

He picks up a note off the floor.

HARRIS (reading)
"Dear Harris, I tried to reach you but your machine
doesn't work sometimes. If you remember I gave
you this door and when we split up you said I

could have it back so I got some people to move
it. Sorry for the inconvenience. Your friend,
Trudi." She took my door.

INT. SARA'S APARTMENT—NIGHT
She dials on her speakerphone. A woman answers.

> SARA

Mom?

> MOM

Hello darling! How are you?

> SARA

What are you doing?

> MOM

I'm making fifty-six papier-mâché hats.

> SARA

Do you feel like playing something?

> MOM

Always darling. The usual?

They begin to play a duet over the speakerphone, MOM on the
piano, SARA on the tuba, playing "Doo Wah Diddy."

INT./EXT.—MONTAGE
HARRIS asleep intercut with shots of the freeway with cars puls-
ing along through the interchange intercut with shots of SARA
playing the tuba with her mother over the speakerphone.

> SARA

Good night, Mom.

INT. SARA'S APARTMENT—DAY

She tosses the dart at the board. It lands four feet to the left of the new position, in the pinned-up photo of HARRIS stumbling.

EXT. BEVERLY HILLS STREET—DAY

HARRIS, in his car, searching out Sara's address. The sound of the tuba wafts throughout the neighborhood.

EXT. SARA'S APARTMENT—DAY

HARRIS waits at the door; SARA answers it. HARRIS sees the tuba inside the door. SARA is oddly distant.

> HARRIS
>
> You play the tuba?

> SARA
>
> I used to. You're late.

> HARRIS
>
> I know. Thank you. It's the new, more liberated, daring, wild me.

> SARA
>
> You work very hard at being liberated, daring, and wild.

> HARRIS (*puzzled by the barb*)
> What did you do? Come to your senses?

> SARA
>
> Maybe. All I know is that your car started moving and ten minutes later your tongue was in my mouth.

> HARRIS (*on his back*)
> I didn't put my tongue in your mouth. That was a lozenge.

EXT. GAS STATION—DAY

They are at a gas station. She's peculiarly icy.

> HARRIS
>
> What is the matter with you?

> SARA
>
> I can't afford this right now.

> HARRIS
>
> How can you not afford it when it's not costing
> you anything?

> SARA
>
> These things don't happen to me. I gave in to
> craziness last night and it shouldn't have happened.
> I've come eight thousand miles and I feel like I'm
> ten years old living with my lunatic family again. I
> have struggled to stay sane all my life, so don't say
> it's not costing me anything.

> HARRIS
>
> Why can't you just relax and be eccentric?

> SARA
>
> Why can't you just relax and be normal? Why is it
> so difficult for you?

> HARRIS
>
> It reminds me that I'm alive.

> SARA
>
> Why don't you just write it on the refrigerator?
> Look, my relationship with my ex-husband is
> proceeding positively and it's something I want to

pursue. I'm really sorry. He might just be the
perfect person.

                    HARRIS
And what is the perfect person?

                    SARA
The perfect person is someone whose faults you
can live with.

                    HARRIS
That's horrible.

                    SARA
Yeah, so is the news I wake up to every morning.

An attendant approaches the car.

                    ATTENDANT
Full-service or self-service, Harris?

                    HARRIS
Full-service, thanks Tony.

The ATTENDANT shouts "full service" at the top of his lungs. Four
Indy 500 tire change pros in gas-station gear come out and change
his tires, lube, and gas him in four seconds.

EXT. DINNER PARTY—NIGHT
HARRIS, SARA and ten others sit at a dinner party. SOMEONE is speaking slowly, monotonously. HARRIS is on the verge of having one
too many.

              BORING SPEAKER (*slowly*)
And I knew it was a great project. If the city were
willing to partially finance my private museum, it

would be a great bonus for the people. So I met
with Ron. . . . Ron, I toast you. . . . (*Toasts.*) And
Ron felt like I did. That the city could be persuaded
to pitch in if . . .

The speech continues. HARRIS starts to look faint. His eyes roll
back in his head.

                    WOMAN
    Are you all right?

                    HARRIS
    I don't know. I feel dizzy.

He starts to collapse. SARA rushes to him.

                    SARA (*concerned*)
    What is it?

                    HARRIS
    I feel a little nausea. If I could get some air.

                    SARA
    I'll take him. . . .

                    GUEST
    You sure?

                    SARA
    Yes.

She escorts him outside.

EXT. HOUSE—NIGHT
They stand poolside in a lush backyard.

HARRIS

It's something in my stomach or head or heart.

SARA

What can I do?

Quickly, he kisses her rather passionately. She responds.

SARA

No, no. I can't do this. This is how Mummy met
Daddy.

She starts to walk away. He grabs her.

HARRIS

Let your mind go and your body will follow.

SARA is stunned that he would say this. How did he know?
There is a noise. They turn. Across the pool, having just
emerged from the foliage, is a deer. HARRIS and SARA stare at
the deer; the deer stares back. It darts back into the night.
The magic of everything makes SARA capitulate. They move
into the foliage.

INT. DINNER PARTY—NIGHT

SPEAKER (*really pompous now*)

. . . to build the greatest private museum in the
world!

HARRIS and SARA reenter.

WOMAN

Do you feel any better?

HARRIS
Much better.

They sit. The WOMAN notices Sara's dress is buttoned one button off in the back.

EXT. MELROSE—NIGHT (OR ANOTHER GREAT LOCATION)
They are walking down Melrose. They stop in front of one of
the neon-lit stores on Melrose. The light flashes on and off behind them.

HARRIS (*v.o.*)
We didn't know what to say to each other so we
wandered down Melrose and had the kind of
small-talk conversation to cover up what had just
happened.

HARRIS
Oh yeah, Harry Zell flew over this morning. The
news wants me back. They want to try the "serious" news and they want me to anchor. You know,
no laughing or chitchat.

HARRIS (*v.o.*)
So there I was jabbering at her about my new job
as a serious newsman, about anything at all, but all
I could think was "wonderful, wonderful, wonderful, wonderful, and most wonderful again."

SARA
I find it difficult to believe the idea of serious news
as a revolutionary concept.

HARRIS
Well this guy does. . . . God you look fantastic. . . .
It'll take some time to get respect after the wacky
weatherman . . . did you, is your hair different?

SARA

The same . . .

Wide shot—the two of them against the neon. The neon flashes: L.A. . . . L.A. . . .

The warm wind comes up. As they walk down the street, the branches in the trees part for them and flowers grow and houses smile. We see them from another angle and they are children dressed in little versions of Harris's and Sara's clothes. Their shoes are too big for them and they walk away from camera holding hands.

INT. HARRIS'S APARTMENT—DAY
HARRIS is busy scrubbing off the "Bored Beyond Belief" sign from his window.

EXT. SANDEE'S HOUSE—DAY
HARRIS arrives at SanDee's house. She is outside waiting with hand luggage. Her boyfriend looks out forlornly from the window. SANDEE is asking HARRIS questions from "Trivial Pursuit."

SANDEE
Who wrote the "Tonight Show Theme"?

HARRIS
Paul Anka.

SANDEE
Good! Hey, where are we going to stay when we get there?

HARRIS
SanDee, I came over here to tell you this. I can't go away with you this weekend.

SANDEE

Shit.

HARRIS

I've been seeing someone and we've got something
going, I don't know what, but it wouldn't be right
for me to go away with you.

SANDEE

Oh, well. So you're seeing her this weekend?

HARRIS

No. I'm not. She's got an obligation to her ex-
husband to see if they can still get it together.

SANDEE

What? She's seeing someone else?

HARRIS

She's going away with him, yeah.

SANDEE

You must be happy about that.

HARRIS

No, I hate it. It drives me crazy. How can she go
away with someone else, especially since I've been
working out.

SANDEE

So you're kind of the jerk who stays home.

HARRIS (*rising anger*)

Yes. But it's fair. It is fair. She had this obligation
before we met.

                    SANDEE
But you had this obligation before you fell for her.
Why should you suffer all weekend?

                    HARRIS
Yeah. . . .

                    SANDEE
So go away with me.

                    HARRIS
I can't. I would only be using you to get even
with her for going off with someone else.

                    SANDEE
I don't mind.

                    HARRIS
Let's go.

                    SANDEE
Great.

                    HARRIS
I thought we'd go to Santa Barbara. The El Pollo
del Mar is supposed to be a nice hotel.

                    SANDEE
Oh, God, it's so beautiful there. There's a million
stars . . . and the beach. I want to spin on the
beach.

                    HARRIS
They have a special spinning beach up there . . .
for nymphets only. (*Then.*) And SanDee, I think it
should be just a vacation, just friends; I don't think
we should make love.

SANDEE

Okay, we'll just have sex. What was Spam Spade's partner's name?

HARRIS

Sam Spade. Archer.

They get in the car.

EXT. SARA'S APARTMENT—DAY

SARA is in the passenger side of a car. The driver's door is open; the trunk is up. SARA is also distracted. There is activity at the trunk, as a few suitcases are being thrown in. Then, the trunk closes and ROLAND gets in the front seat, driver's side.

ROLAND

We might run into people we know at the San Ysidro, so I booked us into the El Pollo del Mar. (*Turns to her.*) I'm really looking forward to this.

He kisses her.

SARA

Me, too.

EXT. VENTURA FREEWAY—HARRIS'S CAR—DAY

Driving toward Santa Barbara. We can hear them playing "Trivial Pursuit" (*voice-over*).

SANDEE (*v.o.*)

What does "lip sync" mean?

HARRIS (*v.o.*)

It's when you mouth a record.

EXT. VENTURA FREEWAY—ROLAND AND SARA—DAY

Driving to Santa Barbara

ROLAND (*v.o.*)

So when the Wittgenstein house was built in
Austria one could say that philosophy of language
had definitely hit the Bauhaus.

SARA

I saw the house a couple of years ago.

ANGLE ON HARRIS'S CAR

SANDEE

Who played "the Beav?"

HARRIS

Jerry Mathers.

ANGLE ON ROLAND'S CAR

SARA

I really prefer the seventeenth-century painted
Italian furniture to anything that was done in
England ever.

ANGLE ON HARRIS'S CAR

SANDEE

Who was Howdy Doody's closest friend?

HARRIS

Buffalo Bob.

INT. EL POLLO DEL MAR HOTEL—DAY

HARRIS and SANDEE are in the lobby checking in. The bellman leads
them off. SANDEE puts her hand on Harris's rear end and he jumps
a little.

INT. EL POLLO DEL MAR HOTEL—DAY (A FEW MINUTES LATER)

SARA and ROLAND are checking in. The bellman leads them off in
similar direction. ROLAND throws his arm around SARA.

INT. HALLWAY OF HOTEL—DAY

HARRIS and SANDEE enter their room. Just as they disappear behind
the door, SARA and ROLAND round the corner and are taken to the
room next to them.

INT. HARRIS'S ROOM—DAY

SANDEE is ecstatic being in the room. She gazes out the window;
she jumps on the bed.

> SANDEE
>
> God, isn't the breeze great?

> HARRIS
>
> It really is nice.

SANDEE rubs up against him. She flops herself on the bed.

> SANDEE
>
> I love hotel sheets. They're so fresh . . . and they
> feel so good against your bare skin . . . oooh.

> HARRIS
>
> I'm putting your toilet bag in here.

> SANDEE
>
> Come here first.

HARRIS benignly comes to her. She gives him a nice kiss and he starts to go back to what he was doing. She hands him champagne.

                              SANDEE
      Come here again.

She takes his hand and puts it down her blouse. HARRIS is reluctantly turned on.

                              HARRIS
      SanDee, your breasts feel weird.

                              SANDEE
      That's 'cause they're real.

SANDEE pulls him to bed.

                              HARRIS
      I should warn you that I'm old and it might take a
      little while. (*after a few seconds*) Oh my God, I'm
      young again!

INT. SARA'S HOTEL ROOM—DAY
They are unpacking.

                              ROLAND
      It's been great to see you again, Sara.

                              SARA
      It's nice to see you, too.

                              ROLAND
      How are you?

SARA

I'm confused.

ROLAND passes close to the wall by the bed.

ROLAND

Hey . . . listen to this . . .

SARA

What?

He puts his ear to the wall.

ROLAND

Listen.

We hear the muffled moans of SANDEE being made love to.

SARA (*put out*)

Oh, Roland. . . .

ROLAND

God, they're going crazy. . . .

It turns him on. He puts his arms around SARA. She reluctantly lets him.

INT. HARRIS'S ROOM—DAY

We see HARRIS and SANDEE in bed making love. Above Harris's head a thought balloon appears. In it is SARA whom he is clearly thinking of. Next, above Sandy's head a thought balloon appears. In it is Mel Gibson.

INT. SARA'S ROOM—DAY

She and ROLAND are making love. Above Sara's head a thought balloon of HARRIS appears. Then, above Roland's head another thought balloon appears. In it is Mel Gibson, too.

INT. HARRIS'S ROOM—DAY

They have just finished making love. SanDee's head is on his chest.

SANDEE

Just before we left Jack told me he wants to make
our relationship exclusive.

HARRIS

You mean he's not going to go out anymore?

SANDEE

I don't think he ever did. He never could get a
date. I think seeing me going out drove him nuts,
too.

HARRIS

What do you think you'll do?

SANDEE

I don't know. I really like him . . . even though he's
not so smart.

HARRIS (*hearing something*)

Hey, listen. . . .

SANDEE

What?

HARRIS

Through the wall . . .

SANDEE

What is it?

HARRIS

Somebody doing it . . .

SANDEE (*delighted*)
Oh . . . how beautiful.

They giggle. We hear Roland's sounds of passion. Roland's bed slams up against the wall several times.

HARRIS
They're really excited; they must be cheating on someone.

EXT. HALLWAY—NIGHT
It is later. HARRIS pops out the door, holding it for SANDEE. They're about to go for dinner. A split second later, SARA opens her door to wait for ROLAND. Harris's and Sara's eyes meet. Then SANDEE walks out and puts her arm around HARRIS. Then ROLAND walks out and throws his arm around SARA.

ROLAND (*seeing Harris*)
My God! I don't believe it! Are you staying here?

HARRIS
Uh . . . yeah.

ROLAND (*friendly*)
Well, SARA, there goes our cover! Ha ha, there's no such thing as a secret.

HARRIS
I think there is. . . . Roland, this is SanDee Wilkes; SanDee, this is Roland Drake and Sara McDowel.

Ad lib hellos.

ROLAND
Where're you headed?

HARRIS

To get some dinner.

ROLAND

That's where we were going. Why don't you
join us?

SANDEE

That'd be neat.

HARRIS

Oh, you might want to be alone. . . .

ROLAND

Don't be silly. We can't both sit in the same restaurant and pretend to be alone . . . come on. . . .

Another angle: SARA and SANDEE are walking together; HARRIS and
ROLAND are walking together. We go with HARRIS and ROLAND.
There is a small clanging sound.

HARRIS

What's that clanging sound?

ROLAND

It's a nuisance. It's my damn testicles.

EXT. BEACH—NIGHT

The four of them walk along the beach. The connection between
HARRIS and SARA is tense. Suddenly SANDEE peels off her top, to re-
veal a bikini top underneath, and begins to spin on the beach.
HARRIS wishes she weren't doing it.

SANDEE

Is it okay to spin here?

HARRIS

Yeah. . . .

SANDEE

Isn't the drive up here great? We played "Trivial Pursuit" the whole way.

ROLAND

What's "Trivial Pursuit"?

SANDEE

It's this great game that has six different categories. . . .

HARRIS and SARA look at each other, hiding their emotions.

SANDEE (*continuing*)

Sports, art, history, literature, and stuff; but we just do the show business ones 'cause the others are so hard. . . .

ROLAND (*to Sara*)

That sounds fantastic. (*Then.*) You want your coat? I'm a little cold.

SARA

Yes I would, thank you.

ROLAND

I'll run up and get them. You want to come, Harris?

HARRIS

Uh . . . yeah . . . uh . . . no . . . I'll just stay here.

ROLAND

Back in a flash.

SARA and HARRIS stand there, finally alone. In the background we see SANDEE dancing in the moonlight.

SARA

You liar.

HARRIS

Here I am innocently driving up to Santa Barbara believing you're seeing your ex-husband and instead you're right next door to me giving it to my best friend.

They are shouting as loud as they can without being heard.

SARA

Your best friend? Since when is Roland your best friend?

HARRIS

He and I are very close. It's a terrible thing for you to do!

SARA

You've never seen him without me.

HARRIS

That doesn't matter. There's a bond among men. Anyway there's two liars here.

SARA

Roland *is* my ex-husband.

HARRIS

Okay, one.

SANDEE (*calling*)

Hey you guys . . . watch.

She does several handsprings.

HARRIS (*calling back*)

Great!

SARA

Why didn't you tell me you just broke up with
someone.

HARRIS

How do you know I just broke up with someone?

SARA

Because when men just break up with someone
they always run around with someone much too
young for them.

HARRIS

She's not so young. She'll be twenty-seven in four
years.

SARA

Jezus, "Seeing your mother" is the oldest cliche
there is. You weren't even clever!

HARRIS

I meant I was seeing my earth mother. (*Then.*) I
told you that because I just couldn't bring myself to
tell you I was going on a weekend with someone

else! I tried to get out of it. I'm up here with her
and all I can think about is you. . . .

SARA

That's why you fucked her this afternoon?

HARRIS

Yes! (*Then.*) I know that doesn't make a lot of
sense. And why me in this? You practically came
through our wall! You know how I felt hearing that
. . . you with someone else?

SARA

You didn't even know it was me till later.

HARRIS

Yeah, but I projected back when I found out.
(*Holding up his fingers.*) This close. We are this
close to it. Stay here in L.A.

SARA (*exasperated*)

What would I do if I stayed? How would it work?

HARRIS

We'd see each other, not push it, take it easy for
the first couple of days, then marriage, kids, old
age, and death.

SARA

And if I were to go?

HARRIS

All I know is that on the day your plane was to
leave . . . if I had the power . . . (*pause*) I would
roll in the fog, I would bring in storms, I would

turn around the magnetism of the earth so com-
passes would not work, so the plane couldn't take
off.

ROLAND appears upon the sidewalk, still thirty seconds away.

> ROLAND (*shouting*)
> Coming!

> SARA (*exhausted*)
> This is everything I didn't want. The pain, the lying,
> the complications; I'm losing control.

ANGLE ON HARRIS: SUPER: TEMPERATURE, 105

ANGLE ON SARA: SUPER: TEMPERATURE, 10
SANDEE walks up.

> SANDEE
> Ever wonder why the water just doesn't fly off into
> the sky?

ROLAND enters with the coats.

> ROLAND
> Here. Now I'm warm from running.

> ROLAND
> Let's walk on down to the pier. . . .

> SANDEE
> Ooooh yes.

Everyone pairs up, SanDee's arm around HARRIS; ROLAND hugging
SARA.

INT. HARRIS'S HOTEL ROOM—NIGHT

SANDEE is nodding off. HARRIS listens very carefully, straining his ear to the wall to try and hear what ROLAND and SARA are doing.

INT. ROLAND'S ROOM—NIGHT

As ROLAND reads, SARA is casually leaning up against the wall, listening to Harris's room.

EXT. HOTEL PARKING LOT—DAY

HARRIS is loading up the car with their luggage.

> HARRIS (*holding up a teddy bear*)
> SanDee, you want this in the trunk or the front?

> SANDEE
> Up front.

She points in her newly learned style. A forlorn ROLAND exits the hotel carrying hand luggage.

> HARRIS (*to Roland*)
> What's the matter? You okay?

> ROLAND
> Huh, sorry. I'm okay. I've been working on Sara to come back with me. I'm her ex-husband. That's the difference between England and America. The English maintain civil relationships with their ex's. Americans kill them. She told me today she doesn't think it's right.

> HARRIS (*up*)
> Really?

> ROLAND
> She's evidently been seeing some American.

115

HARRIS

Well, that's the breaks.

ROLAND

She's not going with him either. She's decided to
go back to London as soon as she can.

HARRIS

Oh.

ROLAND

Pity. I wanted this. I wanted a relationship . . .
you know . . . like you and SanDee have.

EXT. HARRIS'S CAR—DAY

HARRIS and SANDEE are headed back to L.A.

HARRIS (v.o.)

. . . The sun is the center of our solar system,
which is the earth and the other planets. . . . In
turn, the sun is part of a galaxy, which consists of
millions of suns. . . .

EXT. ROLAND'S CAR—DAY

ROLAND and SARA head back.

ROLAND (v.o.)

Who played Fred Mertz?

SARA (v.o.)

How am I supposed to know?

ROLAND (v.o.) (bad pronunciation)

William Frawley.

INT. TV STUDIO—DAY
HARRIS just finishing his serious news report.

>HARRIS
>
>. . . and that man's lawn will probably never grow
>again because of the thoughtlessness of a few
>teenage boys. And here's Morris Frost with a movie
>review.

MORRIS FROST starts a movie review. He is very serious and
"thought provoking."

>MORRIS
>
>The film "Slice up Mommy" is an effort to inter-
>twine the psychological nature of film with the
>tangible experience of storytelling. It starts with a
>slasher, but one whose slashing comes from a
>wound so deep in himself . . .

INT. CAR RENTAL—DAY
SARA drives up to a car rental location.

>SARA
>
>I'd like to turn this car in, please.

INT. TV STUDIO—DAY

>MORRIS (*continuing*)
>
>I give it an eight for content, a six for stylistic
>imagination, a four for eloquence, a six for the
>performances, and a two for relevance.

A chart is supered on the screen, plotting the graph of his
review.

MORRIS (*continuing*)
. . . giving it a mean score of five.

The camera widens to reveal HARRIS listening intently with a "serious" look on his face. He looks an extra long time, giving the seriousness of it all time to sink in. Then very solemnly he says:

HARRIS
And now the weather.

ANGLE ON THE TV
There's a new weatherman. Boston accent. Fifty. Glasses. Serious.

NEW WEATHERMAN
Sunny. Seventy-two. And that's the weather.

INT. CAR RENTAL—DAY
SARA at the check-in counter. A TV is on near the desk.

HARRIS (*on TV*)
Our next weather report will be four days from now. We'll be right back after this message.

INT. TV STUDIO HALLWAY—DAY
HARRIS walks by his boss, TOD, who is choosing rings from a traveling jewelry salesman.

TOD
Harris, it seemed a bit wacky.

HARRIS
What? How could it? I was very serious.

TOD
It had an edge of wackiness. Less wacky, more egghead.

INT. SARA'S APARTMENT—DAY

In a barren apartment, SARA is putting the last of her clothes in a suitcase. Suddenly, HARRIS bursts in. He is talking very fast.

HARRIS

I've been thinking about myself and I think I can become the kind of person that's worth you staying for. First of all I'm a man who can cry. Now it's true it's usually when I've hurt myself but it's a start. You see, I know there is something that will make you stay. I know it. I see you play the tuba I sensed that about you. There is some move I could make, the right word, attitude, plan, but these are all tricks; these are just things I would think up and try. But let's forgo that. Let's assume that whatever that thing is, that whatever it is that you secretly know would make you stay, has occurred, that it has happened, that my hand has already gone down your throat and grabbed your heart and squoze it.

EXT. RESTAURANT—DUSK

SARA exits a restaurant with ARIEL and her new friend ALICE. HARRIS appears, walking beside them.

HARRIS

I am very disappointed in you. I am disappointed that you have chosen the safe, uncommitted path. I'm glad this happened because it reveals some-thing about you that would only have come out later, that you're a weak person, and frankly I'm not interested in that kind of mentality. I need someone who has a drive, a spark, an ability to feel, yes, that's it, an ability to feel . . .

The three girls get in Sara's car. HARRIS pumps up his roller skates and rolls along beside them as they pull out.

ARIEL

Harris, you are a complete goofus.

HARRIS

. . .If you don't think I should be doing that, I
think a simple life is best, maybe a lifeguard, you
me on the beach, few cares. I could also go for
the hard-driving life, get out there, go gettem
something in business. I know that I could do
anything I set my mind to. . . .

INT. SARA'S HOUSE—DAY

SARA is continuing packing, unplugging the phone, etc. Outside,
we can hear HARRIS raving on.

EXT. SARA'S HOUSE—DAY

HARRIS (*muffled*)

Because there comes a time in everyone's life when
it's now or never, now or never. Let me read to you
from a little book of poems . . . (etc.)

SARA closes her suitcase tight and with finality. She opens a
door with a mirror. We see HARRIS standing outside on the lawn.
He sings, "It's Now or Never." She lowers a blind and shuts
him out.

EXT. SIGN—NIGHT

HARRIS stands at the sign. He is weather-beaten and tired.

HARRIS (*angry*)

It's all over. It's all over. You got me into this.

FREEWAY SIGN (*readout*)

IT WAS THE LEAST I COULD DO

HARRIS
What do you mean by that?

FREEWAY SIGN (*readout*)
AT LEAST U R NOT INDIFFERENT

HARRIS (*shifting*)
It's true. It's true. I'm feeling something.

There's a pause.

FREEWAY SIGN (*readout*)
FEEL THE SILENCE (*The wind blows again and the sign resonates.*) DO U REMEMBER THE MOMENT WHEN U FELL N LOVE WITH HER?

HARRIS
I know exactly when I fell in love with her. We were walking along the street after this party and we were talking about nothing really and . . .

FREEWAY SIGN (*readout*)
NO. NO THAT WASN'T IT AT ALL.

HARRIS
What do you mean? Of course it was. (*Then.*) When was it?

FREEWAY SIGN (*readout*)
IT WAS THE MOMENT OF . . . THE TOUCH.

HARRIS
The touch?

FREEWAY SIGN (*readout*)
REMEMBER?

HARRIS

Where?

FREEWAY SIGN (*readout*)

AT THE RESTAURANT.

HARRIS (*remembers back*)

Huh?

We dissolve to the scene in the very first restaurant where he had lunch with TRUDI and the table for eight. We replay the moment where they all get up to leave, then:

The sound of the movie falls away.

The action moves into a vague slow motion.

A waiter moves through the crowd.

HARRIS approaches SARA to move her out of the waiter's path.

The camera jumps in close on Sara's elbow.

We see faces, details, of the other diners, oblivious to the moment.

We see Harris's hand touch her and gently move her.

Fade back to the freeway sign scene.

HARRIS

My God. It had happened already? At the touch?

FREEWAY SIGN (*readout*)

A TOUCH, A GLANCE, A WORD. IT'S ALWAYS FROM THE BLIND SIDE.

HARRIS

Anyway, it's out of my hands now. I did everything I could think of.

FREEWAY SIGN (*readout*)
MAYBE U THINK 2 MUCH.

He turns to go to his car.

FREEWAY SIGN (*readout*)
HARRIS, DID U LOOK AT THAT SIGN I ASKED U ABOUT?

HARRIS
Yes I did.

FREEWAY SIGN (*readout*)
WELL?

HARRIS
Well, you know, pole, recently painted . . . new lettering . . . kinda green.

FREEWAY SIGN (*readout*)
WOW. DID SHE HAVE ALL HER BULBS?

HARRIS
Uh . . . come to think of it she did.

FREEWAY SIGN (*readout*)
THANKS. NOW I HAVE AN IMAGE OF HER.

INT. HARRIS'S APARTMENT—NIGHT
HARRIS sits, raw, in silence.

EXT. SARA'S APARTMENT—NIGHT
A taxi picks her up.

INT. HARRIS'S APARTMENT—NIGHT
He sits and stares at a clock.

EXT. AIRPORT—NIGHT

SARA gets out of the taxi, lugging her tuba.

INT. AIRPORT—NIGHT

She checks in, leaving her tuba at the baggage check-in.

INT. HARRIS'S APARTMENT—NIGHT

He sits. The Rousseau behind him moves slightly. Was it the painting or the shadow of leaves through the window?

INT. AIRPORT LOUNGE—NIGHT

Sara's plane is called.

EXT. FREEWAY SIGN—NIGHT

The freeway sign blinks, electrostatically.

EXT. L.A. STREET—NIGHT

Very still. Everything is very still. A crumpled newspaper in the middle of the street does not move.

INT. AIRPLANE—NIGHT

SARA sits in the plane at the gate. The engines are roaring.

INT. HARRIS'S APARTMENT—NIGHT

He sits.

MONTAGE—NIGHT

The wind blows gently through a palm tree.

The freeways seem empty.

various shots of L.A. Everything is dead, unmoving, like the air before a tornado.

EXT. AIRPLANE—NIGHT

It taxis from the gate.

INT. AIRPLANE—NIGHT

The plane is still taxiing. We see SARA, deep in thought. Outside the window, we see a dense fog cover the window.

EXT. AIRPLANE—NIGHT

The fog envelops the taxiing airplane.

INT. COCKPIT—NIGHT

The PILOT looks at his compass. He taps it.

                              PILOT
        Funny . . .

INT. HARRIS'S HOUSE—NIGHT

HARRIS notices the fog outside his window. A driving downpour begins.

EXT. AIRPLANE—NIGHT

The plane, just yards away from the ramp, is enveloped in rain and fog.

INT. AIRPLANE—NIGHT

SARA. Wondering.

INT. HARRIS'S APARTMENT—NIGHT

Harris's electronic note taker melts.

INT. COCKPIT—NIGHT

Close-up: The pilot's hand throws several switches.

INT. AIRPLANE—NIGHT

SARA hears the sound of the engines shutting down.
Tears come to her eyes.

EXT. FREEWAY SIGN—NIGHT

We see the sign through the mist. Its screen glows dimly, as bolts of light shoot weakly across it, bulbs popping.

EXT. HARRIS'S APARTMENT—NIGHT

He wanders out the door-less apartment. HARRIS stands outside in the rain.

> HARRIS
>
> That's twice.

EXT. HARRIS'S APARTMENT—NIGHT

Sara's taxi pulls up in front of Harris's house. She gets out and faces him in the rain with her bags and tuba. They hug as the clouds reveal the full moon. We see a quick cut of the sign: a digital cloud moves across its screen and reveals the digital moon.

> SARA
>
> It's not going to be easy.

> HARRIS
>
> I'm not really looking for easy.

> HARRIS (v.o.)
>
> Forget for this moment the smog and the cars and the restaurants and the skating and remember only this—a kiss may not be the truth, but it is what we wish were true.

Fade out and up:

EXT. DIGITAL FREEWAY SIGN—NIGHT

HARRY ZELL is hovering in his jet pack in front of the sign, which is now more tattered than it was.

> HARRY ZELL
>
> Goddamn it! I'm working on a deal, this guy wants fifty percent of the overseas. I tell him I can't give him fifty percent of the overseas, I'll look like an idiot!

FREEWAY SIGN (*readout*)
UH HUH

His car phone rings. He answers it, listens for a moment.

HARRY ZELL
Hello? Damn it! (*To sign.*) I'll come back tomorrow at five or else it'll be after eight.

He flies off. HARRIS and SARA pull up and get out of the car. They
walk toward the sign.

HARRIS (*to the sign*)
Wow. That was something. That was really something.

SARA
Yes, it was. Harris explained it to me in the car.
Something to write home about.

The sign gets a surge of energy. A bagpipe sound emerges from
its guts.

FREEWAY SIGN (*readout*)
IT WORKED?

SARA takes her plane ticket and places at the base of the sign.

HARRIS
I always thought it was my fault that I could never
get close to anybody. But now I realize that I had
just always been with the wrong girl.

The bagpipe sound becomes a tune: Amazing Grace.

FREEWAY SIGN (*readout*)

HOORAY FOR US

HARRIS

I never could figure out the riddle though.

FREEWAY SIGN (*readout*)

YOU WILL KNOW WHAT TO DO WHEN U UN-
SCRAMBLE HOW DADDY IS DOING.

HARRIS

Yes. (*To Sara.*) It's a riddle. Too tough for me.

She looks at the riddle. Then:

SARA

I can solve it. It's a British crossword clue. Unscramble means you unscramble the letters of "how
is daddy doing." Okay, we unscramble "how is
daddy doing." Move the "s" and the "ing" . . .

She continues to tell the sign where to move the letters. They
begin to form words. We finally see the sign.

FREEWAY SIGN (*readout*)

SING DOO WAH DIDDY (*Then.*) CONGRATULA-
TIONS!

HARRIS

Sing doo wah diddy? That's the mystery of the ages?

FREEWAY SIGN (*readout*)

I HAD 2 THINK UP SOMETHING FAST.

HARRIS

I sat up nights working on that!

FREEWAY SIGN (*readout*)
HARRIS, ONE OTHER THING.

HARRIS
Yes?

FREEWAY SIGN (*readout*)
THOSE MOUNTAINS . . . WHAT'S ON THE
OTHER SIDE OF THEM?

HARRIS
Oh . . . nothing.

He looks over embarrassedly to SARA. He walks over to the sign
and hugs it. The music generated by the sign multiplies into a
thousand pipes; it's the other freeway signs of the city joining in.

HARRIS
Hey, you got your voice back.

FREEWAY SIGN (*readout*)
REMEMBER. THERE ARE MORE THINGS N
HEAVEN AND EARTH HARRIS THAN ARE
DREAMT OF N YOUR PHILOSOPHY. CONDI-
TION CLEAR.

Sign plays amazing grace.

HARRIS (*v.o.*)
There are only two things in my life I will never
forget. One is that there is someone for everyone.
Even if you need a pick axe, a compass, and night
goggles to find them. And the other is tonight,
when I learned that romance does exist deep in
the heart of L.A.

THE END

Roxanne

The cast of Roxanne *includes:*

C. D. Bales	Steve Martin
Roxanne	Daryl Hannah
Chris	Rick Rossovich
Dixie	Shelley Duvall
Chuck	John Kapelos
Mayor Deebs	Fred Willard
Dean	Max Alexander
Andy	Michael J. Pollard
Ralston	Steve Mittleman
Jerry	Damon Wayans
Trent	Matt Lattanzi

Directed by	Fred Schepisi
Screenplay by	Steve Martin,
	from the play *Cyrano de Bergerac,*
	by Edmund Rostand
Director of Photography	Ian Baker
Edited by	John Scott
Music by	Bruce Smeaton
Production Designer	Jack DeGovia
Produced by	Michael Rachmil and Daniel Melnick

EXT. C.D. BALES'S HOUSE—NELSON, WASHINGTON—DUSK
Establishing. A man exits.

EXT. STREET—DUSK
We are on a busy street in the ski resort town of Nelson, Washington. We see a man walking jauntily and singing "I'm walkin'." It is C.D. BALES. He is wearing a uniform of some sort. Is he a policeman? Postman? From around the corner, FOUR OLDER WOMEN cross the street carrying a TV set.

                    DOTTIE
    Shit!

                    SOPHIE
    Goddamn it!

                    C.D.
    Need some help, ladies?

                    LYDIA
    No thanks. We've got it.

                    SOPHIE
    My electricity blew out.

                    NINA
    We've got three minutes to get this thing to a plug.

                    DOTTIE
    It's *Dallas* night.

                    C.D.
    I thought it wasn't on tonight. I was feeling for you.

                    DOTTIE
    Huh?

SOPHIE (*angry*)
It's a preempt.

LYDIA (*dawning on her*)
He's right. It's that news special on hunger. . . .

The energy drains from their bodies.

NINA
I'm depressed.

DOTTIE
What should we do?

SOPHIE
Let's go get something to eat.

A snazzy sports car rounds the corner; C.D. calls hello to the driver, MAYOR DEEBS, a man who thinks he's Don Johnson: one-day growth, sleeves pushed up (possibly collar up, too).

MAYOR DEEBS
What's happening, C.D.? Looking good; looking very good.

C.D.
Congratulations, Mayor! It was a close race but you won. . . .

MAYOR
Well, no one likes to see their opponent die a week before the election . . . but it's still a victory.

C.D.
So the recount is final then?

                    MAYOR
A buck a year from now on.

                    C.D. (*mutters*)
. . . Overpaid . . .

                    MAYOR
Gonna be a big summer this year . . . tourists up
the wazoo. Got a lot of ideas . . . big ideas for this
town.

C.D. turns a corner. Then, a voice . . .

                    VOICE (*offscreen*)
Hey . . . other side of the street . . . out of the way.

We see down the street, TWO BIG DRUNKEN MEN. They are in tennis gear; one carries a tennis racquet, the other, skis and poles.
They are exactly the types one can see in a macho resort town
on Saturday night.

                    DRUNK
It's a cop.

                    DRUNK #2
If he's a cop, where's his gun? (*Walks up to him.*)
He's a fireman.

They laugh.

                    DRUNK
Cut a wide swathe, pussy.

                    C.D. (*mulling it, then*)
All right . . . all right.

We have never seen C.D.'s face except straight on. He starts to
pass by them.

> DRUNK
>
> Thanks, ass-wipe.

C.D. ignores this too. As he passes them, they look at him, amazed.
They stare for a second. Then one of them says:

> DRUNK
>
> Christ, that's the biggest . . .

But C.D. puts up his hand, abruptly stopping him.

> C.D.
>
> Don't say it.

He moves on. The drunks stare.

> DRUNK
>
> That's quite a hood ornament.

This stops C.D. Something comes over him. Hate. Anger. He turns
to the drunks.

> C.D.
>
> I really admire your shoes.

> DRUNK
>
> What?

> C.D.
>
> I love your shoes.

> DRUNK #2
>
> What do you mean?

C.D.

And I was just thinking that, as much as I really
admire your shoes, and as much as I would love to
have a pair just like them, I really wouldn't want to
be in your shoes at this particular time and place.

The two drunks advance on him. C.D. takes a karate stance. But
so do the other two. C.D. laughs.

C.D. (*continuing*)

I don't really know karate.

DRUNK

I didn't think so.

They relax their stance. Suddenly, WHAM! He karates both of
them. They fall back, shocked. One of them picks up a ski pole.
It is dangerous. He makes stabbing motions at C.D., who maneu-
vers around and manages to pick up the tennis racquet. C.D.
skillfully thwarts every lunge with the ski pole by using the tennis racquet like a fencing foil, intermittently thwacking them on
the head.

The second drunk bear hugs C.D. But he pokes him in the eye
with his nose. Both of the drunks fall back and swoon in pain.

C.D.

Game.

C.D. walks off.

C.D. (*continuing*)

Let's play again sometime.

INT. DIXIE'S CAFE—DUSK

C.D. enters and hands the tennis racquet to Dixie.

C.D.

Where's Dixie? Here's my racket.

WAITRESS
What's this stuff on it, Vitalis?

C.D.
Oh no, that's blood. Where's my tea?

WAITRESS
Ernie . . . you want to tell me about it?

C.D.
Oh no, you're too young.

INT. HOUSE—DUSK

The clock reads 9:30 P.M. ROXANNE KOWALSKI, in her bathrobe, is in the kitchen of a Victorian house. In her late twenties, she is young enough to be beautiful and old enough to be interesting. She is quiet. She is intense, but has a physical silence. Perhaps something has happened to her that makes her pensive.

Her beauty is not a model's beauty. It's the beauty we see in someone at the second glance. The woman who turns you around from the inside, after hours, or maybe days have gone by. Right now, dressed in her bathrobe, she is looking up at the sky. Not longingly, but curiously, as if she were looking for something. Suddenly we hear, from outdoors, the whine of a cat.

ROXANNE
. . . Oh God, Grover! Grover, where have you been?

She goes over to the door and opens it. A blast of icy cold air hits her and she shivers.

ROXANNE (continuing)
Goddamn it's freezing! (Calls the cat.) Grover! Grover!

138

The cat sits tauntingly out of her reach.

                    ROXANNE (*continuing*)
    Grover!

She steps outside the door, holding it open with one foot. Her breath fogs up in the cold.

                    ROXANNE
    Damn you, Grover. . . .

The cat still sits calmly staring at her. She leans forward toward it, her foot loses its grip on the door, and it slams shut. She tries the door. It's locked.

                    ROXANNE (*continuing*)
    Shit!

She is freezing cold, jumping up and down to warm herself.

                    ROXANNE (*continuing*)
    Grover, I'm going around to the front door . . .
    don't go anywhere.

She starts to go, but we see that her robe is caught in the door. She struggles with it, but it is no use. Still freezing, she looks around into the darkness and sees no one, so she slips out of her robe and is stark naked. She runs around to the front of the house and tries the door; it too is locked.

                    ROXANNE (*continuing*)
    Oh God! . . .

EXT. NELSON FIRE STATION—NIGHT—ESTABLISHING

C.D. rounds the corner and walks toward the station.

INT. FIRE STATION—TRUCK ROOM—NIGHT

Three men (RALSTON, CHUCK, and TRENT) are alone downstairs. RALSTON is carrying a bunch of oily rags.

RALSTON

Trent, what should I do with these?

TRENT

Put them in that can.

They drop the rags in a can. Then from upstairs:

DEAN

Come on guys, we're waiting for you.

The men run upstairs. JERRY appears from the bathroom, lights a cigarette, and tosses the match in the can.

INT. FIRE STATION UPSTAIRS—NIGHT

RALSTON, CHUCK, and TRENT rush up the stairs. JERRY appears last. In the background, we see ANDY attempting to put out a fire in the kitchen. He signals to JERRY, who rushes to his aid. Meanwhile, the others are engaged in a game of table tennis. Suddenly, a dilapidated shortwave radio squeals in the background. Its shriek is so piercing that all four men fall to their knees, like it was a death ray on the Starship Enterprise.

DEAN

Turn it off!

TRENT twiddles some dials—Italian emanates from the radio. Smoke starts to appear from the pole hole below.

EXT. ROXANNE'S HOUSE—NIGHT

Still naked, she tries the other doors and window. They too are all locked.

INT. FIREHOUSE—MAIN FLOOR—NIGHT

The men stand up, ready to resume their table-tennis game. C.D.
walks into the fire station and hears a ruckus from upstairs. From
downstairs, the firemen hear C.D. yelling.

> C.D.
> We're not supposed to start them!

The men rush to peer down through the pole hole. C.D. lectures them as he calmly moves to the nearby post and lifts the
fire hydrant from its holder. He looks at the fire and then back
at the men, who all shrug noncommitally.

> C.D.
> Look, I have a dream. It's not a big dream. Just a
> little one.

Casually, he extinguishes the fire and then continues circling
below the pole hole as he lectures.

> C.D. (*continuing*)
> I would like the people in this community to feel
> that if, God forbid, there was a fire, calling the fire
> department would actually be a wise thing to do!
> You can't have people saying as their houses are
> burning down, "Whatever you do, don't call the fire
> department!" That would be bad.

The men peer down, shamefaced. They are interrupted by a
knock from an exterior door.

> C.D. (*continuing*)
> Please. Get it cleaned up. Don't make me have to
> explain this.

EXT./INT. FIRE STATION—NIGHT

C.D. opens the firehouse door, but he sees no one.

C.D.

Hello? Fire Department . . . we start them, you put
them out.

We hear Roxanne's voice from behind a large bush.

ROXANNE

I'm locked out of my house.

C.D.

I can get you back in. Come on in; I'll get some
tools.

ROXANNE

I'll stay out here.

C.D.

Okay. (*Starting, then stopping.*) Why are you
standing in that bush?

ROXANNE

I don't have any clothes on.

C.D. looks and can faintly see a naked figure in the bush.

C.D.

I'll get the tools. You want a coat?

ROXANNE

No, I'd really like to stand naked in this bush.

He goes back inside and grabs some tools. One of the firemen
pokes his head downstairs.

DEAN

What is it?

                        C.D.
Oh, somebody locked out of their house.

                        ANDY
Need some help?

                        C.D.
Looks pretty boring. I can take care of it.

EXT. STREET NEAR ROXANNE'S—NIGHT
C.D. hustles down the street. The bushes rustle along beside him
as ROXANNE moves behind them. They keep moving through the
whole conversation.

            ROXANNE (*from behind the bushes*)
Nobody had a coat?

                        C.D.
I thought you said you didn't want a coat.

                    ROXANNE
Why would I not want a coat?

                        C.D.
You said you didn't want a coat.

                    ROXANNE
I was being ironic.

                        C.D.
Oh. Irony. See we don't get that here. We haven't
had any irony up here since '83, when I was the
only practitioner of it. I stopped doing it because I
was tired of being stared at. You really shouldn't
leave your lights on like this when you're locked
out; you waste a lot of electricity. You can hide

                        143

over in that bush over there and I won't see your
nakedness. I noticed you don't have any tattoos. I
think that's a wise choice. I don't think Jackie
Onassis would have gone as far if she'd had an
anchor on her arm.

ROXANNE

Oh brother. (*Then.*) It's over here.

EXT. ROXANNE'S HOUSE—NIGHT

C.D. works on the door with a credit card. ROXANNE is in the background jumping around trying to keep warm.

C.D.

Well, every job has a perfect tool.

ROXANNE

Oh God . . . Oh God . . . Yayayayaya.

C.D.

Would it make you feel better if I was naked too?
Ha-ha. I'm just a nut.

She gives him a weak laugh.

C.D. (*continuing*)

This lock doesn't accept MasterCard. I'll have to use
the old reliable.

He looks around, studying the house, leaps off the balcony onto
a chair. BOING! He's on the roof. Like the human fly, he swiftly
climbs up the side of the house and enters through a balcony
window. ROXANNE begins to put on her robe, even though it's
still caught in the door.

INT. ROXANNE'S UPSTAIRS SITTING ROOM—NIGHT

As C.D. passes through, he peers into Roxanne's bedroom. Inti-

mate things are laid out and he can't help but see them. Photos.
Perfume. Underwear. He takes his time.

> ROXANNE (*v.o.*)
> Hello?

EXT. ROXANNE'S HOUSE—NIGHT
C.D. throws a robe over the balcony.

INT./EXT. ROXANNE'S KITCHEN—NIGHT
He opens the door for her; she rushes past him and disappears.

INT. ROXANNE'S KITCHEN—NIGHT
ROXANNE enters her kitchen. The cat sneaks in when she opens
the door.

> ROXANNE (*yelling*)
> Do you want to come in . . . ?

But she sees he's already in, at the refrigerator, and has prepared
a nice cheese board and sliced apples.

> ROXANNE (*continuing*)
> Oh . . . well. Would you like some wine with your
> nose? Uh . . . cheese?

> C.D.
> Wine would be okay.

They sit at the kitchen table.

> ROXANNE
> Want some crackers or anything?

> C.D.
> This isn't another one of your tricks, is it?

                    ROXANNE
Huh?

She looks at him curiously, then realizes he's joking and laughs
along with him. C.D. looks at her, a disheveled, pretty mess. He
looks around the room and sees her things lying around: a stack
of college books dealing with the sciences, a lap computer. ROXANNE
pours C.D. a glass of wine. While she pours herself a glass, he
struggles with it to avoid his nose. Finally, she turns toward him.

                    ROXANNE
Do you . . .

Before she can finish her last word, C.D. interrupts.

                    C.D.
Do you have a straw?

                    ROXANNE
No . . . I don't.

                    C.D.
Oh . . . okay.

He sticks his nose deep inside the glass and the wine disappears.

                    C.D.
Well, 'a nose by any other name . . .'

                    ROXANNE
'. . . would smell as sweet.'

They laugh. He likes her. She likes him.

                    C.D. (*continuing*)
My name's C.D Bales. You can call me Charlie. I'm
the fire chief.

ROXANNE

I'm Roxanne. Thank you very much for helping
me.

C.D.

I know the lady who owns this house.

ROXANNE

I liked her. She gave me a real good deal for the
summer.

C.D.

Yeah, nice and cheap, I bet.

ROXANNE

Well, it's worth it. This house has a great spot for
this.

She uncovers a five-foot-long telescope in a corner of the kitchen.

C.D.

You must know about NGC 224.

ROXANNE

Yeah. Of course I do.

C.D.

Don't you think they should name heavenly bodies
much more poetically? I like the Sea of Tranquillity,
Saturn and Jupiter, Andromeda. Now they just
number them. NGC 224.

ROXANNE

No. They still have beautiful names. You know
what a muon is? . . .

Muon?

A gluon? . . . a quark?

C.D. (*bluffing*)
I used to. But I forgot.

She picks up a pencil and paper and sits disarmingly close.

ROXANNE
Well, we don't know everything do we? (*Then.*) No one's ever actually seen a quark. But we know they're out there. There's at least six different types: up, down, strange, charmed, bottom, and top. That's their flavor. The top and bottom quarks are the most common. Only unusually exotic collisions can produce the strange and charmed quarks. It's beautiful, don't you think?

C.D.
Yeah. These are heavenly bodies?

ROXANNE
No, they're subatomic particles.

C.D. (*laughs*)
I thought so. What are you looking for?

ROXANNE
I can't tell you.

C.D.
And why is that?

ROXANNE

I can't. It's a secret.

C.D.

I gotcha. I've got a few secrets myself. Well, one.
(*Kidding her.*) One lousy one. Well, none. It
wouldn't have been as good as yours anyway.

ROXANNE takes another drink. The clock strikes eleven.

ROXANNE

So how does a person get to be a fireman?

C.D.

Well, actually, I was in chemistry class and I
smelled smoke. Nobody else smelled it. I kept
insisting that I did. They thought I was just making
a disturbance but sure enough, there was a fire
inside the walls. Everybody got out in time, and I
met the local firemen and I got along with them.
. . . All my friends were becoming drug addicts . . .
and I was swept up into being a fireman because of
my extraordinary . . . gifts. (*Then.*) Did you say
your name was Roxanne?

ROXANNE

Yes.

C.D.

It's very . . . unusual. Pretty . . . there's a name for a
galaxy. (*Then.*) Well, I've got to get back.

ROXANNE

Well, okay. But wish me luck.

                                        C.D.
On?

                                       ROXANNE
Just luck. No, I don't believe in luck. Wish for . . .
something to happen.

                                        C.D.
I know what you mean.

He raises his glass to her and leaves.

EXT. ROXANNE'S HOUSE—NIGHT
C.D. stands outside the house, looking in at ROXANNE turning out
the lamps one by one. The light goes dark on his face.

                                 C.D. (*to himself*)
Roxanne.

EXT. STREET TO FIRE STATION—DAY
Two men walk down the street. One is the slightly scruffy, but
magnetically handsome, CHRIS MACCONNEL. He carries two large
suitcases, a duffel bag, and his fireman's kit. He's wearing a set
of Walkman headphones. CHRIS has a sloppy, casual, natural
beauty that money can't buy. He oozes sexuality.

The other man, CHUCK, who does nothing to help CHRIS with his
bags, is wearing firemen's clothes. He does not ooze a naive
sexuality, his is methodical and premeditated. An attractive girl
passes by.

                                       CHUCK
Gafornasemano.

                                  GIRL (*stopping*)
What?

Steve Martin as Harris Telemacher in *L.A. Story*. *Photo © 1991 Carolco International. All Rights Reserved.*

Harris (Steve Martin) and Trudy (Marilu Henner). *Photo © 1991 Carolco International. All Rights Reserved.*

SanDee (Sarah Jessica Parker) and Harris: "It wouldn't be so bad if you had to come back." *Photo © 1991 Carolco International. All Rights Reserved.*

Roland (Richard E. Grant), Sara (Victoria Tennant), Harris, and Ariel (Susan Forristal). *Photo © 1991 Carolco International. All Rights Reserved.*

On the set of *L.A. Story*. *Photo © 1991 Carolco International. All Rights Reserved.*

"Mind if I spin?" *Photo © 1991 Carolco International. All Rights Reserved.*

"This is way more important than roller-skating." *Photo © 1991 Carolco International. All Rights Reserved.*

"LET YOUR MIND GO AND YOUR BODY WILL FOLLOW." *Photo ©*
1991 Carolco International. All Rights Reserved.

Roxanne's stars: Steve Martin as C.D. Bales and Daryl Hannah as Roxanne.
Photo © 1986 Nippon Film Enterprises. All Rights Reserved. Courtesy of Colombia Pictures.

"And I was just thinking that, as much as I really admire your shoes, and as much as I would love to have a pair just like them, I really wouldn't want to be in your shoes at this particular time and place." *Photo © 1986 Nippon Film Enterprises. All Rights Reserved. Courtesy of Colombia Pictures.*

On the set of *Roxanne* with the director, Fred Schepisi. *Photo © 1986 Nippon Film Enterprises. All Rights Reserved. Courtesy of Colombia Pictures.*

ROXANNE: Think of what you wrote.
CHRIS: Uh . . . I'm trying.

CHUCK (*to girl*)

June, '85.

GIRL

What do you mean?

CHUCK

June, '85. You were playmate of the month, June, '85.

GIRL

No, I wasn't.

CHUCK

That's funny, I thought I recognized your inner-diameter slope.

GIRL

What's that?

CHUCK

That's the part of the back of the leg that curves into your inner thigh.

Disgusted, she walks on. CHUCK looks over at CHRIS.

CHUCK (*to CHRIS*)

Works every time, maestro. I'm calling you maestro because that's what I think you are with the chicks. I've seen them looking at you. Am I right?

No answer. Just confidence.

EXT. FIRE STATION—PRACTICE YARD—DAY

RALSTON and JERRY bring out two hoses from the truck and train them on burning leaves. They order ANDY to turn on the water.

We see water shoot up from the truck and then realize the hose the firemen are carrying are two ends of the same hose.

EXT. FIRE STATION—DAY

CHRIS and CHUCK are walking to the fire station. CHRIS stops to wonder at the water spurting up behind the building. He shakes his head and goes inside.

INT. FIRE STATION—MAIN FLOOR—DAY

DEAN is watching as the MAYOR is being outfitted by a TAILOR. TRENT, while working on the truck, inquires about the mayor's computer chip on his neck chain. It starts DEEBS off on a tirade about the value of being an entrepreneur.

> MAYOR
>
> What's your name?

> TRENT
>
> Trent.

> MAYOR
>
> Here, take one of these.

He hands TRENT a microchip on a chain.

> MAYOR (*continuing*)
>
> These little babies keep me in Rice Krispies and a nice pad in leisure city.

> TRENT
>
> What is it?

> MAYOR
>
> This is what turns the street lights on in New York, Chicago, Dallas.

CHUCK

Hello?

CHUCK and CHRIS enter.

CHUCK *(continuing)*

Hey, everybody, this is our new pro. A real
firefighter.

MAYOR

Welcome aboard, Chris. I'm Mayor Deebs. We
didn't expect you till Monday.

CHRIS

Yeah, I thought I'd come in early and get a good
start.

CHUCK

He's a maniac with the chicks, too.

MAYOR *(introducing them to Chris)*

Dean, Trent, my personal tailor, Sam.

CHUCK

Come on, Chris. I'll show you your room.

MAYOR *(to Chris)*

What do you think, cuffs or no cuffs?

EXT. QUINN'S HOUSE—DAY

We see a wide shot of an eight-year-old chubby boy sitting on
the roof of a house. From this distance, we can only see that he
is very still, staring off calmly. There is commotion in the street.

ANGLE ON

C.D. in conference with the MOTHER.

MRS. QUINN

He went up there before school and won't come
down.

C.D.

I'll see what I can do.

C.D. goes over to the porch and climbs up on the roof of the
house.

EXT. QUINN'S HOUSE—ROOF—DAY

He angles over to the BOY, who is sobbing silently on the roof.

C.D. (*sitting next to him*)

What is it, Peter?

We get the feeling that the BOY trusts C.D.

PETER

They call me Porky at school.

This is familiar territory with C.D., and it hurts him, too. Sitting
beside him, he puts his arm around the BOY.

C.D.

Why do they have to do that? Goddamn it. I
shouldn't say that in front of you. (*Then.*) Do you
ever talk to your mother about it?

PETER

Once I tried, but she said I had to clean up my
plate first.

C.D. looks at the BOY, and the BOY begins to laugh.

                              C.D.

Now see, that's good. You're way better than
those guys who call you names—you're smart and
funny. You can make things up.

                             PETER

I didn't make it up; it's true.

                              C.D.

Oh.

                             PETER

Bastards. I shouldn't say that in front of you. Do I
have to get down now?

                              C.D.

No. No. Hell with 'em. Let's just stay up here for a
while.

They sit in silence, staring out into the sky.

EXT. QUINN'S HOUSE—STREET—DAY
We see a big wide shot of C.D. and the BOY sitting on the roof
with the twenty or so people standing below watching them as
the sun sets behind the house. They do not move. We get the
feeling they are going to be there for hours.

EXT. 279 BAR—ESTABLISHING—NIGHT
ANDY, JERRY, and TRENT enter the bar.

INT. 279 BAR—NIGHT
We are in the 279 Bar. It's a thriving nightclub and great pick-up
spot.

Tonight it's particularly rowdy—there is a brief scuffle in the far
corner. A flashbulb pops somewhere.

ROXANNE and DIXIE are huddling at the bar. DIXIE is a vital busy-
body who knows everyone's business. She is friendly and lik-
able and is just getting to know ROXANNE. SANDY, peppy and flirty,
is tending bar.

DIXIE

Daddy died on the porch, not in the house. . . .
Hey, if you want, I've got an extra Betamax you
can borrow. And I got tons of tapes. If there's
anything you want me to tape, let me know. I tape
Dallas for Sophie and Lydia, and do all the soaps
for C.D. You know what he does with them? He
reedits them. He mixes them all up. They're really
funny.

ROXANNE

He's really funny . . . I think.

DIXIE

Yeah, he's my god-brother. I installed a dish and
now I get everything. When's your boyfriend
coming? What's his name . . . Richard?

She falls silent, then speaks.

ROXANNE

He's . . . not coming. (*Beat.*) We just ran out of gas.
I think I mistook sex for love.

SANDY

I did that once. It was great.

DIXIE

When Jack went nuts and left me, I bought stock in
those lust and love novels . . . actually, I made a
thousand bucks.

She studies ROXANNE a beat, then:

DIXIE (*continuing*)
You feel pretty bad, huh?

ROXANNE
You know what a sail-squirrel is?

DIXIE
It's a squirrel on the road that's been run over so
many times you could pick it up and sail it.

ROXANNE
That's how I felt. (*Then.*) Do you have any aspirin?
I always get a headache for a while at this altitude.

DIXIE
Yeah.

SANDY
Roxanne, all you need to do is get laid about
sixteen times by some of these guys around here.
Just don't mistake it for love.

DIXIE (*fishing in her purse*)
Try a couple of these. My mother sends them to me
from Canada.

ROXANNE (*to Sandy*)
If you're feeling empty, you don't do something
that's going to make you feel emptier.

SANDY
Wow! That's really good advice—logical, reasonable . . . and boring.

SANDY walks away.

DIXIE

Sandy's a very deep person.

ANGLE ON

CHUCK and CHRIS walk into the 279 Bar. They pass the MAYOR, who glad-hands a group at a table.

MAYOR (*to table*)

... No one likes to see an opponent pass away, but ...

CHUCK (*shouting*)

I can lick any girl in the house! (*Then, quiet.*) This uniform. It really works. That's why I'm a volunteer.

ANOTHER ANGLE

They sit. Scanning the room, he spots ROXANNE.

CHUCK

God, who's that. She could certainly make my night.

CHRIS is captivated by her. Roxanne's eyes scan across him too.

CHRIS

Who's she?

CHUCK calls over SANDY, the barmaid, who is passing by with drinks.

CHUCK

Hey, Sandy, who's that?

That's Roxanne. She writes books on astronomy or
astrology or something.

CHUCK

There's a difference?

ANGLE ON

ROXANNE's table. SANDY, returning to the bar, points out CHRIS to
ROXANNE.

SANDY (*noticing Chris*)

Who's that? God. He could cheer you up.

CHRIS, again looking swell and in control, drinks his beer.

CHUCK (*to Chris*)

Look, someone's looking at you.

He indicates ROXANNE. She is indeed looking at him, out of the
corner of her eye.

CHUCK

If I was you, I'd do something about that.

CHRIS

Maybe. Maybe later. Maybe not.

CHUCK

You're playing it beautifully. You don't mind if I
give it a shot.

He gets up and walks toward ROXANNE. CHRIS watches him, then
gets up and follows.

CHUCK approaches. He is disgustingly overcasual.

CHUCK

I'd like to invite you to a Nelson tradition of hot-tubbing.

ROXANNE

Pardon me?

CHUCK

It's kind of a tradition here to have mulled wine and then some outdoor hot-tubbing.

ROXANNE

Tradition? You mean the settlers came here a hundred years ago and started hot-tubbing?

CHUCK

Huh?

DIXIE

You have a hot tub?

CHUCK

Oh yeah. Well, a friend of mine does, but I'm getting one.

ROXANNE

How long has he had it?

DIXIE

Three months.

ROXANNE

So this is a tradition that really started about three months ago.

CHUCK

Hey, you're feisty. I like that.

On that line, she looks glumly at SANDY. She turns back to CHUCK.

ROXANNE

I'm sorry. But I just have to stop talking now.

CHUCK

Tell you what. I'll be over there . . . (*To Sandy.*) Sandy, fix her up with a mulled wine . . . (*Back to Roxanne.*) . . . and you start thinking about it and just come on over if you change your mind. And I think you might.

ROXANNE

Well, if I do change my mind, you'll be able to tell because my breasts will be heaving and moist with perspiration.

CHUCK

So long, foxy.

ROXANNE

So long.

CHUCK

Later.

CHUCK swaggers back to his table.

ROXANNE

So this is what it's going to be like being single.

SANDY

He's got a great ass.

ROXANNE

Yeah. Too bad it's on his shoulders.

SANDY

He's cute.

DIXIE

He's a flirt. Waste of space.

ROXANNE

Listen, I have nothing against cute; I just . . . God,
I'd love to meet someone with half a brain this
time.

CHRIS, who has been standing by overhearing all this, is drawn
up short. At that moment, Roxanne's head turns and stares straight
into his eyes. There is indeed a moment of "Some Enchanted
Evening."

ROXANNE

Hello.

He stands silent, trying to talk to her; however, he is unable to
speak. In fact, he is petrified. But in his stupor, with the light
falling on him so his already handsome features are accentuated,
he looks more sophisticated and intelligent than he really is.
Finally, his confusion and fear drive him away, perspiring. He
panics and leaves the club.

162

ANGLE ON ROXANNE

We see ROXANNE, who watches CHRIS exit. She is obviously taken
with him.

EXT. 279 BAR—NIGHT

CHRIS flies out of the door and throws up around the corner of
the building.

INT. FIRE STATION—UPSTAIRS—DAY

CHRIS is examining the computer being installed by TRENT. Noise
emanates from the computer.

> TRENT (*pointing*)
> Look, there's a fire . . .

> CHRIS
> . . . in Los Angeles.

ANDY enters.

> ANDY
> That's our new computer. We can pinpoint any fire
> in town with that. It's perfect for us because, you
> know, we're the fire department.

> CHRIS
> That *is* perfect.

> ANDY
> How are you?

> CHRIS
> Fine. I'm fine.

> ANDY
> So I just wanted to welcome you.

CHRIS

Okay, thanks.

ANDY

So, okay. (*Starts to go, then*) Hey, there is one thing.

CHRIS

Yeah?

ANDY

You met the chief?

CHRIS

No.

ANDY

Well, he's kind of, you know, funny looking. So, uh, I wouldn't mention it.

CHRIS

I wouldn't do that.

ANDY

Yeah, I figured that. But sometimes something can accidentally slip out and then, you know . . . (*making throat-slitting gesture.*)

CHRIS eyes him curiously.

INT. ROXANNE'S HOUSE—DAY
C.D. and ROXANNE are carrying the telescope up the stairs.

C.D.

Thank God I have a counterbalance. Why is this thing so heavy? It's mostly air.

ROXANNE

Yeah, and glass, so just be careful!

C.D.

I had an aunt who knitted one of these once . . . it
was much lighter than this.

They start to position the telescope.

C.D.

This secret of yours . . . it relates to this thing?
Right?

ROXANNE

Yes.

C.D.

Then I feel I have a right to know what it is. Now. I
don't want you to tell me, but if you don't, I'll kill
you. No, I wouldn't do that . . . I would have you
killed.

ROXANNE leans close—teasingly sultry.

ROXANNE

If you really want to know, I think I've discovered
a comet. It's no big deal, there's lots of comets. . . .
(*She gets more serious.*) I was working on a paper
on the Oort cloud which involved checking
through old records of comets and I noticed a
mathematical irregularity . . . I have a knack for
that . . . but it was a consistent irregularity. I think
what people believe are ten comets are actually
one. Probably pulled out of its orbit by the gravita-
tional pull of a planet.

So what do you get if you're right?

Well . . . nothing. I'd graduate, that's for sure. And I'd get to name it.

Well that's pretty good . . . sort of historical.

Yeah. "Kowalski's Comet."

God. Kowalski!? Why? You've got a chance to give it a beautiful name.

That's my name.

Roxanne Kowalski? I would go the more conventional route . . . something like Louie, Tony, Tiny, Trent . . .

I could call it Trent if I wanted.

How about something in an international vein like Pepe? . . . or Wong the Comet?

They laugh.

When do you find out about this thing?

ROXANNE

July 14, six P.M. EST, give or take 10 days either
side. That's when I figure it's due back.

C.D.

That would really be something.

INT./EXT. CHAMELEON CAFE—DAY

ROXANNE sits at a cafe with DIXIE and SANDY. This restaurant is loud
and they must practically scream their dialogue.

SANDY (*biting into a burger, yelling*)

I love this thing.

DIXIE (*yelling*)

I love having an intimate lunch!

A Chinese waiter approaches. He asks them something, in English, but his accent and the noise make it impossible to understand.

DIXIE (*yelling*)

Yes!

SANDY

What did he want?

She makes an "I don't know" gesture. Behind them, the MAYOR,
with TRUDY in tow, has stopped to work the room. ROXANNE, who
has been sitting quietly throughout, finally speaks.

ROXANNE

What's the point?

SANDY

Excuse me?

ROXANNE

What's the point of meeting this guy? What if he's
a jerk?

DIXIE

Who?

ROXANNE

This guy . . . from last night.

SANDY

She's never going to meet anyone ever again
because they might be a jerk. . . . So he's a jerk!
You get rid of him! . . . I mean after you lay down
with him for a couple of weeks.

DIXIE

I'm shocked.

ROXANNE

Yes. We're all tremendously shocked.

DIXIE

I know I am. Hey, don't look now but the viking
just came in.

SANDY

Jesus, it's him.

ANGLE ON ROXANNE'S TABLE

SANDY

He should be bronzed. Roxanne, it's now or never.

ROXANNE

Oh Sandy.

SANDY

Do it, Roxanne. What difference does it make?

ROXANNE

Maybe you're right. I'll get him out of my system.
When he comes out I'll invite him for a Nelson
tradition of hot-tubbing.

They laugh. CHRIS disappears inside the men's room.

INT. CHAMELEON CAFE—REST ROOM—DAY

CHRIS is inside, standing nervously. He turns on the faucet to wash
his hands, but turns it a little too hard. The water splashes up on
his trousers in a most conspicuous place, leaving a large, embarrassing stain. CHRIS is horrified. He tries to remove the stain
with a towel—no luck.

ANGLE ON ROXANNE'S TABLE

The three women watch the door.

ANGLE INSIDE REST ROOM

The windowless bathroom is empty. No CHRIS. High up, a nar-
row vent is open. How did he get through it?

EXT. FIRE STATION—DAY

CHRIS walks up to the station in stained pants and enters.

EXT. STREET—"ALL THINGS DEAD"—DAY

ROXANNE passes by. CHUCK notices her and advances. Although it's
an eighty-degree day, he wears a lavish fur coat.

CHUCK

Anything catch your fancy?

ROXANNE turns toward him.

                              ROXANNE
Hi.

                              CHUCK
Hi, remember me?

                              ROXANNE
I'm trying to put it behind me. This is your shop?

                              CHUCK
Yeah.

                              ROXANNE
It's just so perfect. You. This shop. It's a perfect
match.

She walks on. C.D. stares at her from the window of an antique
shop. He picks a hideous object out of the window.

                          SHOP OWNER
Why are you buying this?

                              C.D.
To get it out of your window. I have to pass by
here every day.

ANGLE ON ROXANNE
She walks down the street. But it's *her* walk (slightly slo-mo?).
She is exquisite. Sensual. The sun glints off her hair. It's a powerful
moment for C.D.

EXT.—STREET—DAY
He sheepishly gets in the truck and drives off. At that moment,
the MAYOR and DEAN walk down the street, leading a cow.

                    MAYOR
Well, it came to me. In a flash. Last night.

                    C.D.
What is that?

                    MAYOR
The gimmick. The thing. The Nelson promotional
cow. We think up a name, Suzie, Bossy, Esmerelda.
We put her picture up in the corner of all our
posters, drinking a beer. Everywhere. These things
work. It works for the Olympics, it'll work for us.

                    C.D.
That's a terrific idea. Great. Absolutely great . . .

C.D. wanders off, muttering.

                C.D. (*continuing*)
. . . What an idea. Genius . . . an idea whose time
has come . . . (etc.)

INT. FIRE STATION—UPSTAIRS—DAY
CHRIS, by the hose-drying tower, is approached by DEAN, who
introduces himself.

                    DEAN
It's nice to have you here.

                    CHRIS
Thanks. You got a nice station here.

                    DEAN
Yeah. (*Pointing.*) Hey, great stain! . . . Sorry. The
chief's desperate for someone like you. See, the
other guys are just amateurs. I am too but I have

more of a feel for it than they do. You can imagine how worried he was with just me and him to really handle the place.

CHRIS

Is there a lot of, you know, fires here?

DEAN

Well, we had one, awhile ago, 1887. Some jerk left a cow in a barn with a lantern. Dumb. Dumb thing to do. Same thing happened in Chicago but they got all the publicity. Where you from?

CHRIS

Albuquerque.

DEAN

Oh yeah? Can you spell it?

CHRIS

Yeah.

DEAN

So can I. (*Then.*) Say, one thing. Have you seen the chief?

CHRIS

No.

DEAN

Yeah. Well, he's kind of sensitive about . . .

CHRIS

I heard. He's funny looking or something?

                              DEAN
Yeah.

                              CHRIS
What is it? What's he look like?

                              DEAN
He's got . . . (*Looks around, nervous.*) He's got . . .

He looks around the station making sure he's alone.

                         DEAN (*continuing*)
This incredible honker. Whatever you do, don't say
anything. . . .

                              CHRIS
I wouldn't do that. . . .

                              DEAN
When I saw him I nearly died. I had to get out of
the room. I didn't mean too. I just looked at him
and all I could see was nose.

                         CHRIS (*worried*)
Oh God.

INT. FIRE STATION—DAY
JERRY is polishing the truck. He is annoyed as a greasy TRENT pushes
past, leaving a skid mark. RALSTON leans on a nearby post holding the polish can. CHRIS shuffles into the fire station.

                             RALSTON
You must be Chris.

                              CHRIS
Yeah.

                              173

RALSTON

I'm Monitor Ralston. I just go by Ralston. People
never heard of Monitor as a first name and it saves
me having to explain it. What a bore. So call me
Ralston.

CHRIS

Nice to meet you, Ralston.

JERRY

Hi! I'm Jerry. You met C.D.?

CHRIS

The fire chief? No.

RALSTON

There's something you should know.

CHRIS

He's got a big nose.

The volume worries RALSTON and JERRY. He looks around nervously.

RALSTON

Whatever you do, don't stare.

CHRIS

Look. Look, I wouldn't. I wouldn't stare.

JERRY

Yeah. None of us would. But you get there, and
you feel yourself not staring.

RALSTON

Then you think, "It's obvious I'm not staring," so
you look. Then you think, "I'm staring." So you say,

this is ridiculous. So you take a good look and
you realize here's a guy when he washes his face
he probably loses the soap.

The others react nervously to the joke.

                    CHRIS
Oh no. . . .

EXT. 279 BAR—ESTABLISHING—NIGHT
ANDY, CHUCK, and a WOMAN enter the bar. (Possibility of showing
C.D. entering and exiting bar.)

INT. 279 BAR—NIGHT

ANGLE ON
C.D. sits in a far corner of the bar, meeting with MAYOR DEEBS.

                    MAYOR
. . . Charlie, this town can be like Aspen. You
know how much money they're making?

                    C.D.
A million dollars a minute. I don't know. Look . . .
you can't run a fire department with the four
banana brothers. You need professionals. . . .

                    MAYOR
You got a professional coming. . . .

                    C.D.
So that'll make two experts at putting them out
and four experts at starting them.

                    MAYOR
Once the Octoberfest promotion is over, then we
can see about getting the funds back to you. . . .

Have you seen the new "You Are Here" maps
around town? They're a tremendous hit. . . .

C.D.

Octoberfest . . . I don't get it. It's not even October. This is July!

MAYOR

It doesn't matter what month it is. It's what it
represents . . . it could be April.

C.D.

So, "It's like October in July."

MAYOR

Yeah. Great slogan! (*To Dean.*) Write that down.
(*Then, to C.D. again.*) Then, in the fall, we could
have Cinco de Mayo. Hey! (*He moves off.*) Nobody
likes to see an opponent pass away.

In the background, a flashbulb pops again. Meanwhile, JIM, at a
table with RALSTON and JERRY, has been observing C.D.

JIM

What the hell is that?

RALSTON looks up and sees C.D. walking to ROXANNE and Dixie's
table.

RALSTON

That's C.D. Bales. He's . . .

JIM

What's that on his face?

176

RALSTON
That's his . . . his . . .

JIM
Nose?

RALSTON
Shhhh . . . don't mention it. One word . . . a look,
mention anything long or in the general vicinity of
. . . (*makes nose gesture*) . . . and you have to deal
with him.

JIM
You do, huh.

ANGLE ON
The bar. JIM approaches C.D. looking to have some fun.

JIM
I heard you're tough.

C.D.
I am. But if you use a little tenderizer I might cook
up pretty good.

JIM
Asshole . . .

C.D. (*playing to the crowd*)
Well, now he's going to want to know who I am.

C.D. walks away.

JIM
Where do you think you're going, big nose?

There is an audible gasp from the crowd.

C.D.
Pardon me?

JIM
You heard me . . . big nose.

C.D.'s face makes a visible, frightening change.

C.D. (*calmly*)
Really.

JIM
Yeah.

C.D.
Is that all?

JIM
Well, yeah.

C.D.
Well, you really got me on that one.

He starts to walk away.

C.D. (*continuing*)
Uh . . . wait a second. God, what a waste of an
opportunity.

JIM
What?

C.D.

Well, I mean you've got a guy standing in front of you with this . . .

He indicates his nose.

C.D. (*continuing*)
. . . and all you can think of is "Big Nose."

JIM

I suppose you could think up something better?

C.D. (*he hands him a dart*)
. . . take this. Whatever number you land on, that's how many I'll think up.

JIM expertly throws the dart. It lands on twenty.

C.D.

Twenty? Shit. Two out of three.

JIM throws the dart again. It hits twenty. C.D. moans.

JIM

Denver Darts Champion. 1987.

C.D.

All right, twenty something betters. Here goes. Let's start with . . . Obvious: Is that your nose or did a bus park on your face? Meteorological: Everybody take cover. She's going to blow. Sad: Oh, why the long face? Deductive: With an eraser like that, there must be a mighty big pencil around here some-where. Helpful: If you got some handles for that thing, you'd have a nice set of luggage. (*With a lisp, moving to the bar.*) Fashionable: You know, it might deemphasize your nose if you wore something larger, like Wyoming. Snide: Table for two? Personal: Well, here we are, just the three of us. Punctual: All right, Delman, your nose was on time, but *you* were fifteen minutes late! Instructive: No, you've got it wrong: Let a *smile* be your umbrella. Envious: Oh, I wish I were you! To be able to smell your own ear. (*Moves to Roxanne's table.*) Naughty: Pardon me sir, some of the ladies have asked if you'd mind putting that thing away. . . . Philosophical: You know, it's not the size of a nose that's important, it's what's in it that matters. . . . Humorous: Laugh and the world laughs with you; sneeze and it's good-bye Seattle. Commercial: Hi, I'm Earl Schieb and I can paint that nose for thirty-nine ninety-five. . . . Polite: Would mind not bobbing your head; the orchestra keeps changing tempo. Melodic: (*singing*) He's got the whole world, in his nose. . . . Sympathetic: What happened? Did your parents lose a bet with God? . . . Complimentary: you must *love* the little birdies to give them this to perch on. . . . Curious: When you sleep facedown, what does it do, retract? Scientific: Hey, does that thing there influence the tides? Obscure: Whew, I'd hate to see the grindstone. Inquiring: When you stop and smell the flowers, are they afraid? French: The pigs have refused to find any more truffles until you leave! Pornographic: Now here's a man who can satisfy two women at once. Familiar: Aren't you the great prognosticator, Nostrildamus? (*To the crowd.*) How many is that?

The answer is quick from an enthusiastic TRENT, who watches with ANDY.

TRENT

Fourteen . . .

C.D. shoots him a look.

C.D.

God . . . (*Then.*) Religious: The Lord giveth . . . and
he just kept on giving.

CROWD

Fifteen!

C.D.

Disgusting: Who mows your nose hair?

CROWD

Sixteen!

C.D.

Paranoid: Keep that man away from my cocaine!

CROWD

Seventeen!

C.D.

Aromatic: It must be wonderful to wake up and
smell the coffee in the morning . . . in Brazil.

CROWD

Eighteen!

C.D.

Appreciative: How original. Most people just have
their *teeth* capped.

CROWD

Nineteen!

C.D. (*after some thought*)
Dirty: Your name wouldn't be Dick, would it?

CROWD

Twenty!

The crowd cheers.

JIM

You smart-ass son-of-a-bitch.

C.D.

You flat-faced, flat-nosed, flathead.

C.D. sticks his nose out, daring him to hit it. JIM takes a swipe at him, but C.D. dodges it and trips him gracefully. JIM gets up, takes a swing, but C.D. takes one slug and walks away, knowing he's dropped him.

EXT. 279 BAR—NIGHT
C.D. exits, whistling down the street.

INT. STATIONERY STORE—DAY
CHRIS enters and goes to the counter.

CHRIS

Did that copy of *Being in Nothingness* by Jean-Paul
Sartre arrive yet?

CLERK

Yes it did. I've got it right here.

We see ROXANNE with her back to CHRIS, looking at a book. She turns and sees the clerk hand the book to CHRIS.

CLERK

It's all paid for.

CHRIS leaves the store.

EXT. STATIONERY STORE—DAY

CHRIS hands the book to ANDY. (JERRY and RALSTON could be passing by. Also possibly SANDY?)

ANDY

Thanks. I was embarrassed to ask for it myself.

EXT. DIXIE'S CAFE—ESTABLISHING—DAY

The BIDDIES enter the cafe.

INT. DIXIE'S CAFE—DAY

Dixie's Cafe is the hangout for locals. Huge breakfasts of pecan waffles. The camera passes JERRY, with TRENT and DEAN, in the throes of ordering from an impatient RALSTON.

RALSTON

The usual, guys?

RALSTON tries to remain cool as he is barraged with a huge and diverse order by all three. Each of the guys is very hungry and very particular. RALSTON hates it.

ANGLE ON

DIXIE sitting with C.D. DIXIE is holding the *Wall Street Journal*.

DIXIE

Condex is at fourteen and three-quarters.

C.D.

Ouch! We should sell that.

DIXIE

Dristan's up a point. Whoah, Kleenex leaped to 27.

C.D.

Yeah. I had a cold last week. It'll go back down.

DIXIE

You know, I got $7,500 for my house!

C.D.

Which one, of the five.

DIXIE

The one down on Rush Street.

C.D.

Oh yeah. Where Roxanne is.

DIXIE

How well do you know her?

C.D.

Ran into her a couple of times. With you.

DIXIE

Do you like her?

C.D.

Yeah.

DIXIE

She needs something to brighten her up a little.
She's bummed. Why don't you ask her out?

C.D.

I'd have to try and fit her in. I've got a three
o'clock, I've got a five o'clock. The women are
always around driving me nuts. Mostly because of
the old saying . . .

He spots SOPHIE, one of the four older ladies, at the counter.

C.D.

Sophie, you know the old saying about a man's
nose?

SOPHIE

Sure, you mean how the size of a man's nose
relates to the size of . . .

She takes a look at C.D.'s nose.

SOPHIE

. . . Oh my God. . . .

The other BIDDIES "oooh" as well.

DIXIE

Why don't you take her out?

C.D.

You know, sometimes I just walk around at night
and I see couples walking along holding hands and
I look at them and I think, Hey, why not me. And
then I catch my shadow on the wall.

C.D. taps his nose in reply. There is a silence. DIXIE leans in to
him.

DIXIE

Why don't you just get that nose job?

                              C.D.
I did.

                             DIXIE
Oh.

                              C.D.
Besides, the word is so terrible: rhinoplasty. It has
the same pleasant ring as "hemorrhoid." There're
two words you just don't want to be involved with.

                             DIXIE
Well, maybe some cosmetics, you know, a little
shading or something. It really helps.

DIXIE indicates where to apply blush.

                              C.D.
No, no, no, no, no, no.

SANDY, the bartender from last night, approaches the table.

                            SANDY
Hi.

                             DIXIE
Hi, Sandy.

                        SANDY (to C.D.)
God, were we impressed with you last night.
Especially Roxanne. She went on and on about
you.

                              C.D.
She did?

                              186

Yeah. And I think she fell in love, too; she just
doesn't know it yet.

SANDY moves on, leaving C.D. to wonder.

C.D.

What did she mean, "She thinks she fell in love?"

DIXIE (*kidding him*)

Oh, she's probably just interested in you sexually.

C.D. (*equally kidding, making a funny voice*)

Ugh. That would be terrible.

EXT. FIRE STATION FORECOURT—DAY

C.D. enters the fire station.

INT. FIRE STATION—DAY

C.D. walks in. TRENT works on the truck. ANDY helps. CHUCK is in
the background folding hoses. They suspiciously stop what they
are doing. C.D. heads up the stairs, not quite sure what's going
on. The firemen are nervous. Not laughing.

ANDY

I'll go get him.

C.D.

Who?

ANDY

The new guy.

C.D.

Okay. Hi Dean.

> DEAN (*polishing the fire pole*)

Hi.

> C.D. (*to Trent*)

Hi Trent.

> TRENT (*from under a truck*)

Hey, Chief.

> C.D.

Hi, Chuck.

> CHUCK

Nice shirt. Looking good.

> C.D. (*climbing stairs*)

Thanks.

As C.D. begins to climb the stairs, all the men turn away. On the eighth step, C.D. pretends to run upstairs. Immediately, CHUCK, ANDY, TRENT, and DEAN snap their heads toward the staircase from which C.D. glares. He's caught them.

EXT. PRACTICE YARD—DAY

ANDY approaches where CHRIS is nervously pacing.

> ANDY

He's here. Don't panic.

> CHRIS

Oh God.

INT. FIRE STATION—UPSTAIRS—DAY

RALSTON and JERRY play pool. C.D. goes into the kitchen to get a banana.

Oh, hi, C.D.

C.D. (*loudly*)

Hi!!!

ANDY

Chris, this is C.D. Bales. Chief, this is Chris
MacConnel.

ANDY backs out of the way, his eyes glued to the action. CHRIS is
desperately trying to control himself.

C.D.

Welcome. We can use you around here.

Elongated shot of C.D.'s nose whipping through the air as he
turns around.

CHRIS (*biting his tongue*)

It's great to know you, too. Well, got a lot of work
to do.

C.D.

Okay. See you later.

He turns away. Then turns back.

C.D.

Bye-bye.

CHRIS

I just want you to know that I'm not . . . you know,
looking. But it's not that I'm not looking. I am
looking . . . just the right amount. Not too much,
not too little.

C.D.

Well, why are you looking?

CHRIS

Uh . . .

C.D.

Are you disgusted by it?

CHRIS

. . . No . . .

C.D.

Is there a fly on it?

CHRIS

No . . .

C.D.

Well then, it couldn't be that you find it perhaps
just a trifle large?

CHRIS

No. It's small . . . real small—Tiny . . . teeny-weeny.
Itsy-bitsy!

C.D.

No. It's LARGE.

CHRIS

No it isn't.

C.D.

Yes it is.

CHRIS
I mean large. God, it's big! *It's huge!*

The firemen disappear. "He's going to kill him, there'll be nothing left," etc. C.D. advances on CHRIS. CHRIS mutters things like, "I'm sorry, they told me not to, I can't help it," etc. The firemen react alarmed.

C.D.
Want a sandwich?

CHRIS
Huh?

C.D.
Want a sandwich or anything?

C.D. moves over to the kitchen, resuming his salad. Curious beyond belief, CHRIS walks over to him.

CHRIS
Excuse me. But these guys said you'd go nuts if I said anything about . . . it.

C.D.
Ordinarily, yes. But not today.

CHRIS
So what's different about today?

C.D.
Yesterday, she didn't. But today, she does.

CHRIS nods appreciation. He smiles at him. C.D. smiles back. They begin to laugh.

ANGLE ON THE FIREMEN

They peer through the pole hole. The fireman enter the room.

DEAN

Hey, you've finally got a sense of humor about it.

DEAN laughs merrily. C.D. slams him up against the wall in two moves.

EXT. STREET—DAY

DIXIE and ROXANNE, in Dixie's all-black Blazer, with tinted windows, pass by C.D., who's talking to CHUCK and possibly JERRY. The truck backs up and ROXANNE gets out.

ROXANNE

Can I see you?

EXT. SKI LIFT AREA—DAY

ROXANNE and C.D. amble up the hill. They are alone.

ROXANNE

What I'm going to say is a little forward.

C.D.

Good.

ROXANNE

There's someone I think I should get to know better.

C.D.

Yes. . . .

ROXANNE

Someone who I think likes me, too. You know what I mean?

C.D.

Yes. . . .

ROXANNE

I think he wants to talk to me. . . . I can see him trying. But he won't. I like him for that.

C.D.

Maybe he needs you to make the first move.

ROXANNE

That's why I'm talking to you.

C.D. (*convinced it's he*)

Well. And what else do you know about him?

ROXANNE

All I know is he's interesting.

C.D.

Uh huh. . . .

ROXANNE

. . . different . . .

C.D.

Yeah. . . .

C.D. gets more carried away with each adjective.

ROXANNE (*continuing*)

. . . handsome.

C.D. (*stopped dead*)

He's what?

ROXANNE

Handsome.

C.D.

It's amazing if you have feelings for someone how
you can start to see them as handsome.

ROXANNE

Well, everyone thinks he is.

C.D.

Not everyone . . . believe me. . . .

ROXANNE

What are you talking about?

C.D. (*realizing*)

Nothing. It's just great that he's all these things.

ROXANNE

I've only seen him twice. We've never even spo-
ken. Just exchanged a couple of goofy looks.

C.D.

So why are you telling me this?

ROXANNE

Because he works for you. His name is Chris
MacConnel.

C.D.

Oh, yeah . . .

ROXANNE

What's he like? No, don't tell me. Let's just let it
happen. Since you're going to be working with

him, I thought you could encourage him. Not too
much, just enough.

He thinks about this a long while.

>ROXANNE (*continuing*)
He might not say anything all summer, and then I'll
be gone.

>C.D.
Well, if it comes up.

>ROXANNE
Thanks, C.D. I know I'm forward. (*She kisses him on
the cheek.*) You were great the other night. It was
the first time I've ever seen anyone actually be
brave.

>C.D.
Listen, I've been a lot braver since then.

EXT. DOCTOR'S OFFICE—ESTABLISHING—DAY

INT. DOCTOR'S OFFICE—DAY
C.D. is with a doctor, the local cosmetic surgeon.

>C.D.
This time I want to do it, Frank. Cut the thing off.

>DOCTOR
C.D., you know I can't.

>C.D.
You've got to.

DOCTOR

C.D., you can't. You know that. You've been in comas before. Allergies to anesthetics are very serious.

C.D.

So we do it without the anesthetic.

DOCTOR

That's impossible. The pain would be unbearable. You'd go into shock.

C.D. (*he sees himself in the mirror*)

I always thought I could stand it.

DOCTOR (*sitting down, man to man*)

You know, C.D., all these things against you— maybe you were born with a nose for a reason.

C.D.

You mean like opening Coke bottles?

DOCTOR

Maybe it's some sort of a test.

C.D.

I don't want a test.

He puts his face in his hands. However, his nose gets slightly in the way.

C.D.

Frank, could I look at the nose cards one more time?

DOCTOR (*sympathetically*)

Sure.

He hands C.D. a stack of cards, each one graphically showing
different types of perfect noses. C.D. holds one at a time up to
his face, swooning over them like a kid in a candy store.

EXT. STREET—DAY
C.D. and CHRIS walk along the street. CHRIS is in torment.

CHRIS

Roxanne, she wants to meet me?

C.D.

That's right! Oh, lucky man!

CHRIS

That's fantastic! That's great! She was *the* most
beautiful girl there. She's really beautiful.

C.D.

She's interesting, too. . . .

CHRIS

Interesting? Did you see her legs?

C.D.

She's also got a sense of humor.

CHRIS

I can't believe it! God, she wants to meet me! I
heard she was smart, too, astrology or something.

C.D.

Astronomy . . . yeah.

CHRIS

That's great. God, she wants to meet *me*? So
what'll I do?

C.D.

Huh?

CHRIS

So what do I do? How do I meet her?

C.D.

I don't know. She's around. Walk up to her on the
street.

CHRIS

No, I'd have to talk to her.

C.D.

What are you talking about?

CHRIS

Look, around you guys I can relax, I can be myself.
I'm funny. You know I'm funny. But I get around
women and I get nervous. It's not that I don't like
women. I like women! I like women! But I just get
a little nervous.

C.D.

Okay. So get her number and call her.

CHRIS

Pass. Then I'd really have to talk to her. I wanted
to talk to her the other night, real bad, but I
didn't 'cause that's how I would've talked to her.
Bad.

                              C.D.

So every time you run across a woman with a
little charm, style, legs—you're going to back off
and just run in the other direction?

                              CHRIS

What a great idea.

NINA, SOPHIE, DOTTIE, and LYDIA turn the corner, marching somewhere. They are wearing tennis gear, holding racquets, and
sweating profusely.

                              NINA

. . . Sophie, you can't be my partner anymore. You
miss the easy ones.

                              SOPHIE

You're insufferable.

                              DOTTIE

I hate tennis.

                              NINA

It's a dumb game. Why do we even play?

                              C.D.

Must have been a tough game, ladies.

                              NINA

We're just on our way there.

They pass by.

                              C.D.

Chris, do you know what carpe diem is?

                              199

CHRIS

Is that a fish?

C.D.

It's Latin. It means, "Seize the day." It means there
may not be a tomorrow. It means seek life now. Do
it now, while you're young. While you have the
chance.

CHRIS

So you think I should go after Roxanne?

C.D.

No. Not at all. I'd wait. Mail her a letter.

The fire alarm sounds. They race to the station.

EXT. FIRE STATION TOWER—DAY

Close-up of tower with mountains in background.

INT. FIRE STATION—DAY

C.D. arrives simultaneously with CHRIS.

C.D.

Go upstairs and find out where it is. I'll wait here
for the men.

INT. FIRE STATION—DAY

CHRIS races up the stairs.

INT/EXT. FIRE STATION—DAY

C.D. waits outside, looking impatiently down the street for the
volunteers. Momentarily, CHRIS emerges.

CHRIS

False alarm. Goof up in the computer. Nothing.

> C.D.
> Well, we'll see how long it takes them to get here.

FOUR CUTS:

C.D. waiting. And waiting. Finally, ANDY, TRENT, and CHUCK amble up. RALSTON being dropped off by his wife, JERRY walking, eating a sandwich, etc. C.D. does the slow burn.

MAYOR DEEBS, with DEAN, screeches up in his Porsche. DEAN gets out. C.D. excuses the MAYOR, who drives off.

EXT. BEHIND FIRE STATION—DAY

The firemen stand at attention, slightly scared, like they've just been read out. C.D. is about to give a demonstration of controlled burning. A pile of old mattresses sits in the middle of a vacant yard. He walks around a minute, checking all the gear. Then:

> C.D.
> Okay. Light the thing and we'll see how you do.

One of the firemen approaches the mattresses. He lights a match. C.D. spots CHRIS just inside the station, behaving erratically. He is singing to himself and laughing. He goes in for a moment to talk to him.

> CHRIS
> Hey, C.D., come here. Chief, come here. I've got it.

> C.D.
> I had it once, but I got rid of it.

Throughout this speech, we can see the firemen in the background trying to light the fire. They can't.

> CHRIS
> I know how to talk to Roxanne. You're right. I'm going to take a chance. Now here's a girl who

201

likes me. And what am I afraid of her for? She's
no rocket scientist. . . .

                    C.D.
She is a rocket scientist.

                    CHRIS
Oh. . . . Yeah but, out of all the guys in this town,
she likes me, right? You said so. So what have I got
to be afraid of? Nothing! So what I'm going to do is
what you said, write her a letter. I've got a way
with words. Ask these guys. I entertain them all the
time. See, this way, I can plan out what I'm going
to say. I can craft it. In a letter, I can be . . .
effergoddamnvescent.

ANDY enters.

                    ANDY
Chief, we can't get the damn thing started.

                    C.D.
I'll be out in a second.

                    ANDY
Thanks.

He turns to go. C.D. stops him.

                    C.D.
Andy.

                    ANDY
Yeah?

C.D.

Your coat's on fire.

Indeed, Andy's coat is burning.

ANDY

Uh . . . thanks.

He pats out the flames.

CHRIS

So what do you think?

C.D. thinking, surveys everything around him: CHRIS, the firemen, everything. He speaks like he's just turned into Norman
Bates.

C.D.

I think it's a wonderful day. I love the sky today,
don't you? Oh my, look at the clouds. . . .

He wanders outside. CHRIS stares at him.

EXT. STATIONERY STORE—DAY

From across the street, we see CHRIS enter.

INT. STATIONERY STORE—DAY

CHRIS is buying supplies. We get the feeling he has never been in
a stationery store in his life, but he is exuberant.

CHRIS

I'm planning to write a letter.

MARSHA

Yes.

                              CHRIS
So I would like the necessary equipment.

                              MARSHA
Ah. Well, you'd need a pencil. . . .

                              CHRIS
I would like to buy a pencil.

                              MARSHA
Yes sir. Anything else? Paper?

                              CHRIS
Uh, yes. A piece of paper.

                              MARSHA
A piece of paper? Just one?

                              CHRIS
Better make it two.

                              MARSHA
Okay. A pencil and two pieces of paper.

                              CHRIS
And I'll buy an envelope, too.

She hands over the goods and watches curiously as CHRIS
departs.

INT./DRUGSTORE—DAY
C.D. shops. The clerk, CYNDY, approaches.

                              CYNDY
Hi, C.D.

C.D. turns; caught.

                              204

C.D.

Hi.

CYNDY

Can I help you?

C.D.

I have a friend who was looking for a cosmetic or wondering if one exists, sort of a shading type of arrangement. Do you have anything like that that would be a shading kind of thing?

CYNDY

Well, we have lots of blushes and things. What specifically was it for?

C.D.

She has this feature that she would like to deemphasize.

CYNDY

I see. She's got this feature that she'd like to make look smaller.

C.D.

Exactly.

CYNDY

I think what you've got would be fine.

C.D.

How would she apply this thing?

CYNDY

She would just shade the area of the feature to appear that there are more shadows and less actual acreage . . . uh, area.

C.D.

I'll take it. I'll take it.

CYNDY

Okay. I'll get a fresh one from the back.

C.D.

Thanks.

ROXANNE is by C.D. in the store.

ROXANNE

Hi, Charlie.

C.D.

Hi. I talked to Chris for you.

ROXANNE

Great. Do you think he's going to call me or something?

C.D.

He wants to write you a letter.

ROXANNE

A letter. Isn't that usually what you do at the end of a relationship?

C.D.

No, actually, it's really romantic when you think about . . . (*Tries to get Roxanne out of the store before Cyndy comes back.*) I'll explain it to you outside if you want. . . .

CYNDY

C.D., here's your blush.

C.D.

Uh, yes. Could you gift wrap it?

CYNDY

Uh, sure.

She exits.

ROXANNE

Got a girlfriend?

C.D.

It's for my sister.

ROXANNE

Oh, you have a sister?

C.D.

Well, I don't. It's really for my sister's girlfriend.

INT. STATIONERY STORE—DAY

CHRIS is at the stationery store again.

CHRIS

I'd like more paper, maybe ten sheets, and a pencil
sharpener.

MARSHA

Ten sheets of paper, comin' up!

INT. CHRIS'S ROOM—DAY

CHRIS sits by the window struggling enthusiastically with his letter.

INT. C.D.'S HOUSE—BATHROOM—NIGHT

C.D. is alone in his apartment, opening a box of blush. He ex-
periments with it in front of a mirror but gives up quickly. The
phone rings.

                              C.D.
Hello? Sure Chris, I was just making some eggs.

INT. C.D.'S HOUSE—LIVING ROOM/KITCHEN—NIGHT

CHRIS is in C.D.'s room, showing him his letter.

                            CHRIS
I thought I better show it to you before I send it.

                       C.D. (*reading aloud*)
"Dear Roxanne, how's it going? Want to have a
drink sometime? If you do, check this box." (*Turning to Chris.*) How long did you work on this?

                            CHRIS
Since noon.

                              C.D.
Chris, that is a very long time. You want something
to eat?

                            CHRIS
Sure.

The scene continues as C.D. cooks something wonderful in the
kitchen. He looks at the pathetic, hopeful CHRIS.

                              C.D.
You can't send her this. Look, do it this way.

He takes out a pen and paper and gives them to CHRIS.

                       C.D. (*continuing*)
How do you feel about her?

                              CHRIS
Me? About her?

A look of exasperation crosses C.D.'s face.

                              C.D.
Yes. How did you feel when you first saw her?

                              CHRIS
Horny.

                              C.D.
Okay. But you can't write, "I felt horny when I first
saw you." Say, "I felt moved, alive, on fire. . . ."

                              CHRIS
God, that's beautiful.

CHRIS writes it on the paper.

                              C.D.
Now, how did you feel when you first tried to
speak to her?

                              CHRIS
Like a goddamn idiot.

                              C.D.
Okay. But instead of saying, "I felt like a goddamn
idiot," let's say, "I was mute, dumb, unable to form
words."

                              CHRIS
. . . mute, dumb, unable to form words.

CHRIS writes that down on the paper.

C.D.

And what did you do after you saw her?

CHRIS

I puked.

C.D.

Hmmmm. "After seeing you, my only nourishment was you."

CHRIS

Hey, C.D. You write the letter. This is fantastic, C.D. Come on, you can do it. You know what to say. You know how to say the things I feel. You write it, I'll sign it.

C.D.

That's lying.

CHRIS

Not if you write what I feel. I'll just sign my name. You write to Roxanne what you would imagine I'm feeling.

C.D. (*considering it*)

. What I would imagine you're feeling?

CHRIS

Yes. You've already gotten it half written anyway.

C.D.

No, I don't. I wouldn't write this . . . this is just sort of poetic baloney.

CHRIS (*indicating what he's already written*)
This? No, this is beautiful. . . .

C.D.
No. For Roxanne you need something . . . startling.
Something so deeply felt, so direct, that it would
make her incapable of being reasonable.

He pours himself some wine.

CHRIS
Could you do it?

C.D. (*deliberates*)
I think it would be an interesting challenge.

EXT. ROXANNE'S HOUSE—DAY
We are outside her rented Victorian. ROXANNE is at the mailbox
and takes out the letter. She reads it as she walks to the house
and we can see her take halting steps as the letter intrigues her.

DISSOLVE TO:

EXT. LAUNDRY—DAY
C.D. is walking down the street. Turning a corner he sees a curious thing. It's the fire truck parked in a space in the street. He
looks around, trying to figure out what's going on. Finally, RALSTON
enters the street from the dry cleaners carrying his laundry. He
spots C.D.

RALSTON
The wife was using the car.

INT. FIRE STATION—DAY
The phone is ringing as C.D. enters, and he answers it.

Yes ma'am. Right away. That's on Pine, right?

He hangs up and sounds the alarm.

FOUR QUICK CUTS:

INT. RESTAURANT KITCHEN—DAY
Andy's head pops up.

EXT. DIXIE'S CAFE—DAY
Through the window, we see RALSTON, who looks toward the alarm and exits.

EXT. CHUCK'S SHOP—DAY
Through the window, we see CHUCK trying a fur on a lady customer. His head jerks toward the alarm and he exits.

INT. COUNCIL CHAMBERS—DAY
MAYOR DEEBS, addressing the city council, mutters and runs outside.

EXT. STREETS—DAY
The MAYOR is first to arrive in his Porsche. Then, CHUCK, ANDY, DEAN, JERRY, TRENT, and RALSTON hustle toward the fire station.

EXT. FIRE STATION—UPSTAIRS—DAY
They charge up the stairs as C.D. cuts the alarm.

C.D.
Six and a half minutes. All right. It's all right. Now get into your gear. Fast!

The seven volunteers and CHRIS slide down the pole.

INT. FIRE STATION—MAIN FLOOR/LOCKER ROOM—DAY

We see them jump awkwardly into their fire-fighting clothes and assemble by the fire truck.

C.D.

Very good. We've got a cat up a tree at Sophie Pollard's house. Get over there and get it down!

RALSTON

A cat up a tree? I was eating!

MAYOR

I had a meeting.

C.D.

Listen, it could be you up there.

RALSTON

I'm a human. I wouldn't be up a tree. This is only a cat.

C.D. (*chastising him*)

Only a cat. Only a cat. A cute little bundle of meowing fluff. What have you got against Snowball?

MAYOR DEEBS

Who's Snowball?

C.D.

Mrs. Pollard's cat. But in a way Snowball represents all cats. You have a cat, don't you, MAYOR? What's its name?

MAYOR

Puff.

C.D.

Well, this time it's Snowball up there. But one day
it could be Puff. Don't you see? It doesn't matter
who's up there. Puff, Snowball, or Puss-puss. That's
what firemen are all about! Now go!

As the volunteers scramble onto the truck, C.D. indicates to CHRIS
that he's not included in this call.

EXT. FIRE STATION—DAY

C.D. watches the truck scream out of the station.

EXT. RESIDENTIAL STREET—A TABLEAU—DAY

We see a close-up of a cat in a tree. The camera pulls back to
reveal two firemen in the tree, in full uniform, crawling toward
the cat, one fireman hobbling around the ground with a
sprained ankle, and another trying to get the ladder to extend.
It's a real vision of ineptitude. The FOUR OLDER LADIES, including
SOPHIE, look on.

ANOTHER ANGLE

C.D. comes strolling around the corner, sees the sight, and tries
not to wince. He walks up to the tree and opens a can of cat
food while staring glumly at the men.

He sets the can down and we watch the cat work its way down
the tree to it. C.D. turns away and walks back down the street,
shaking his head.

EXT. STREET NEAR FIRE STATION—DAY

C.D. walks back to the station. The fire truck passes him. He looks
at it. Panic crosses his face. He starts to shout.

C.D.

Boys! . . . Boys! . . . The ladder's still up! . . .

He starts to chase after them. We hear, offscreen, a crunching sound.

EXT. FIRE STATION—DAY
C.D. approaches the station.

ANGLE ON THE STATION
The truck is inside the station. The ladder, still attached to the truck, is sticking out through an upstairs window. RALSTON, TRENT, JERRY, ANDY, and DEAN emerge out of the fire house.

> C.D.
> How did you do it?

> RALSTON
> I don't know.

EXT. ROXANNE'S HOUSE—UPPER BALCONY—NIGHT
We see a fabulous shot of Saturn. The camera swings around to the Veil Nebula. We realize we have been looking through a telescope.

> ROXANNE (v.o.)
> Here's the Veil Nebula.

We see DIXIE, ROXANNE, and C.D. gathered around the telescope.

> C.D. (pushing Dixie away)
> You'll see it, you'll see it. (Peering.) It really makes you realize how big we are.

> DIXIE (looking)
> Excuse me. What is it?

> ROXANNE
> It's exploding gas.

DIXIE

I know the feeling.

ROXANNE

God. What a setup. (*Then.*) I want to show you a double binary. See that star up there . . . to the upper left of the bright blue one?

DIXIE

Yeah.

ROXANNE

It's really two stars revolving around each other, but they're so far away they look like one.

She swings the telescope around.

DIXIE

What keeps them together?

ROXANNE (*playful*)

Mutual attraction.

DIXIE

That's fairly romantic.

ROXANNE

Yeah. Strange attracters in my window of possible movement.

C.D. flushes and DIXIE is lost.

DIXIE

Say again?

ROXANNE (*dreamy*)

". . . passionate kisses that I hope you'll read with your lips . . ."

DIXIE

Roxanne.

ROXANNE

Oh, something from a letter I just got.

C.D.

Oh yeah?

ROXANNE

Yes. An amazing letter.

DIXIE

Ooh. I want one.

C.D.

You liked it?

ROXANNE

No, I didn't like it. I loved it.

C.D.

Really. . . .

DIXIE

Whose letter?

ROXANNE

Chris.

DIXIE

He can write?

ROXANNE

I'm melting. (*Back to telescope.*) Let me show you
the Dumbbell Nebula. (*Then.*) . . . But there's
something I don't get. Here's a guy who dodges me
for days. So I think, okay, he's not interested. Then
C.D. tells me he wants to write me a letter and I
figure it's going to be about why he won't talk to
me. But it's not. It was strange and intelligent and
. . . sexual.

DIXIE is intrigued—particularly by C.D.'s odd reaction.

DIXIE

Wait a minute, why's he writing? He only lives a
block and a half away.

ROXANNE

You've seen what happens when I've tried to meet
him. Charlie, would you tell him I've invited him
over to the house?

C.D.

Yeah, sure.

ROXANNE

And if he doesn't show . . . I guess I'll just have a
broken heart.

EXT. FIRE STATION—DAY

C.D. talks to CHRIS. Chris's face lights up.

CHRIS

She wants a date? All because of you, too, you
know. Ooh, that's great!

C.D. watches as CHRIS starts to walk into the firehouse, singing.

CHRIS

I'M LOOKING OVER, A FOUR-LEAF CLOVER . . .

He starts to wheeze. Asthma?

C.D.

What's the matter?

He is frozen in fear.

CHRIS

Tonight? She wants to see me tonight?

C.D.

Yeah . . .

CHRIS

I can't. I'd be a wreck. I'm dying now and it's only
three.

C.D.

You have to relax. Be yourself.

CHRIS

I don't have a self. You got me into this. I didn't
want this.

C.D.

I didn't get you into this.

CHRIS

You've got to help me. I'll die if I have to talk to
her. I'll die.

C.D.

I'll give you something to memorize.

CHRIS

I can't memorize.

C.D.

Of course you can.

CHRIS

I can't.

C.D.

Say the Pledge of Allegiance. You memorized that,
didn't you? Go on.

CHRIS

I pledge allegiance, to the flag of . . . of . . . the
country . . . of . . . I'm nervous!

C.D.

All right. We'll think of something. . . . Relax.

EXT. STREET—ROXANNE'S HOUSE—DUSK
CHRIS walks up.

EXT. ROXANNE'S HOUSE—FRONT PORCH—DUSK
He approaches the door and knocks. ROXANNE answers. CHRIS is
wearing a hunter's cap with flaps down over his ears.

ROXANNE

Hi.

CHRIS (*nervous*)

Hi.

ROXANNE

No letters this time, just face-to-face.

CHRIS

Yeah.

ROXANNE

Want to sit outside?

CHRIS

Do I want to sit outside? (*A pause.*) Yes!

ROXANNE

Here?

CHRIS

Here on the porch? (*A pause.*) Yes.

They sit on the veranda. There is an awkward pause.

ROXANNE

It's a lovely evening, isn't it?

CHRIS

Yes, it is an exquisite evening, filled with mysterious portents. Magic. Romance.

ROXANNE

Why are you wearing that hat?

CHRIS

Why? . . .

EXT. ROXANNE'S STREET—CONTINUOUS ACTION—DUSK

We see a van parked across the street from Roxanne's. The camera moves toward it, and dissolves through.

INT. DIXIE'S TRUCK—DUSK

We see C.D. at a radio transmitter. He is at the mike and speaking into it.

> C.D.
>
> Because tonight, I am a hunter . . . hunting for words.

EXT. ROXANNE'S HOUSE—FRONT PORCH—DUSK
BACK TO CHRIS

> CHRIS
>
> . . . I am a hunter . . . hunting for words.

> ROXANNE (*fencing*)
>
> Am I your prey?

BACK TO C.D.

> C.D.
>
> Yes. But not a defenseless one.

BACK TO CHRIS

> CHRIS
>
> Yes. But not a defenseless one. Not a rabbit. You are a lioness.

BACK TO C.D.

C.D.
Alert and sensitive . . .

BACK TO CHRIS

CHRIS

Alert and sensitive to every misstep.

ROXANNE

I see . . .

CHRIS

I must move silently. Moving in toward you. My
hand outreaching. (*His hand moves toward her
face.*) (*Suddenly.*) Car three, car three, proceed to
the 279 . . .

ROXANNE

What?

INT. DIXIE'S TRUCK—DUSK
C.D. looks curiously at his equipment. We hear . . .

POLICE RADIO VOICE

Car three . . . do you confirm?

C.D. bangs on the equipment.

EXT. ROXANNE'S HOUSE—FRONT PORCH—DUSK
BACK TO SCENE

CHRIS

Do you confirm? Do you confirm?

ROXANNE

Confirm what?

CHRIS (*again on track*)
Confirm my feelings . . .

ROXANNE

Yes.

CHRIS

Because there is a heart here that wants yours
to know that . . . (*suddenly, police voice*) . . .
there is a possible 502 on Main . . . Proceed
to Main.

ROXANNE

What?

INT. DIXIE'S TRUCK—DUSK
ANGLE ON C.D.
He bangs on the radio.

EXT. ROXANNE'S HOUSE—FRONT PORCH—DUSK
BACK TO CHRIS
The radio squeals in his ear; he rips off his hunter's cap.

CHRIS

Sorry. . . .

ROXANNE

You're not a hunter anymore?

CHRIS must now find his own words.

CHRIS

Not a hunter? . . . Not a hunter. . . . Yes . . . I mean
. . . (*quickly changing*) . . . it's nice out, isn't it. . . .

really, really . . . really . . . really, what's the word
I'm thinking of . . . *nice* out.

ROXANNE

So now you're the weatherman. . . .

CHRIS

Huh? . . . Oh! HAHAHAHAHA.

ROXANNE

I loved your letters. It was beautiful. Where did you
learn to write like that?

CHRIS

Oh, you know. The usual places.

ROXANNE

They seem very extemporaneous.

CHRIS (*stumped*)

Thank you.

ROXANNE

Say something, something wonderful like in your
letter.

CHRIS

Well, let's see. Uh . . .

ROXANNE

I know. Tell me what you think of the night.

CHRIS

It's . . . the night is . . . very . . . extemporous.

                    ROXANNE
What?

                    CHRIS (*nonplussed*)
This is wild. (*Then, inspired.*) Love is wild. Wild
and extemperaneous.

                    ROXANNE
Yes. Say something romantic.

                    CHRIS
Why do birds suddenly appear every time you're
near?

                    ROXANNE
Isn't that from a song?

                    CHRIS
Well, they made it into a song.

                    ROXANNE
You wrote the song?

                    CHRIS
No, but I like that song.

                    ROXANNE
Use your own words.

                    CHRIS (*trying hard*)
You . . . you have . . . you have a great . . . body.

ROXANNE is stunned. CHRIS tries again.

CHRIS *(continuing)*

Your . . . your knockers . . . no, not your knockers, breasts! Your breasts are like . . . are like . . . melons . . . !

ROXANNE

What!?

CHRIS

No, not melons . . . pillows . . .

ROXANNE *(doubtful, but listening)*

Yeah . . .

CHRIS

Can I fluff your pillows?

She rises in horror and backs toward the front door, almost crying in her disappointment.

ROXANNE

I have to go in now.

She runs in the house. CHRIS sits stunned on the front porch. He makes one last call to her.

CHRIS

June, '85!

She stops momentarily.

ROXANNE

What?

227

CHRIS

Weren't you the playmate of the month in June,
'85?

ROXANNE, flabbergasted, storms into the house.

EXT. ROXANNE'S STREET—NIGHT
C.D. emerges from the van. He drags CHRIS away from the house.

C.D.

Sorry.

CHRIS

I got flustered! I panicked. You've got to help me!

C.D.

I think it's over, Chris.

CHRIS (*desperate*)

She wants me now. God, why can't I say the right
things.

Roxanne's shadow appears at her upstairs bedroom window. She
is upset, we can tell. And then, with the utter, cold truth, he says:

CHRIS (*continuing*)

She wants someone who looks like me and talks
like you.

C.D. looks up at the window. A daring, unbelievable idea enters his head. He drags CHRIS back to Roxanne's house.

EXT. ROXANNE'S HOUSE—GARDEN—NIGHT

C.D.

Let's give it to her.

CHRIS

Huh?

C.D.

It's pretty dark here.

CHRIS

What are you thinking?

C.D. (*excited*)

You stand over there . . . under the window. I'll
stand here, out of sight.

He stands below the window, hidden from view.

C.D. (*continuing*)

I'll whisper to you what to say. . . .

CHRIS

What if she hears you?

C.D.

Shhh . . . shhh. . . . Call her.

CHRIS (*swept away*)

Roxanne!

C.D.

No, here. . . .

He hands him some pebbles, which CHRIS throws at the window. ROXANNE appears.

ROXANNE (*opening the window*)

Who is it?

CHRIS

It's me. Chris.

ROXANNE

Oh.

She starts to close the window.

CHRIS

I wanted to tell you . . .

He looks desperately at C.D.

ROXANNE

What? That I'm really built?

CHRIS

No, no, not that.

CHRIS dashes frantically to under the balcony where C.D. is standing.

CHRIS (*continuing, to C.D.*)

What should I say?

C.D. (*whispering*)

Tell her that you were an idiot.

CHRIS

What?

C.D. (*urgently*)

Tell her!

He dashes out from under the balcony.

CHRIS (*to Roxanne*)
I was an idiot. . . . (*Still repeating.*) I was a . . .
stupid . . .

C.D. stumbles around underneath the balcony, miming more words.

CHRIS
. . . face-making . . .

C.D. points to his rear end.

CHRIS
. . . pointer?

CHRIS gives C.D. a puzzled look.

ROXANNE
Pointer?

CHRIS finally gets it.

CHRIS
Ass!

ROXANNE
So why did you say those things?

He dashes under the balcony.

CHRIS (*to C.D.*)
Why did I say those things?

C.D. (*whispering*)
You were afraid. . . .

He dashes back.

CHRIS (*to Roxanne*)

I was afraid?

ROXANNE

Of me?

Again, he runs to C.D.

CHRIS (*to C.D.*)

Of her?

C.D.

Tell her you're scared of—

ROXANNE

What do you mean, afraid? Afraid of what?

C.D.

—of words.

CHRIS

Huh?

C.D.

Words!

CHRIS (*not hearing*)

Worms!

C.D. violently pulls CHRIS out of Roxanne's view.

C.D.

Give me your coat.

CHRIS

C.D., this is no good.

But C.D. is yanking him out of his coat, hissing with quiet urgency.

C.D.

Give it to me . . . quick! (*To the closed window.*)
Not worms . . . words! They're hard to say. They've
all been used up.

In shadow, half-hidden by a tree branch, C.D. speaks up to ROXANNE. His voice is conveniently distorted by the breeze.

ROXANNE

I can't hear you.

C.D.

My words have to rise up and they're having
trouble finding you.

ROXANNE

You're not having trouble hearing me.

C.D.

Your voice floats down. But be careful. One hard
word from you at that height kills me.

ROXANNE

Your voice sounds different.

CHRIS

Oh God. . . .

C.D.

Of course it's different! I don't have to be careful
anymore. I'm protected by the night. I can be
myself, Roxanne. God, your name is a knife.

ROXANNE

Stand where I can see you.

CHRIS

NO!

ROXANNE

Why?

He lets out his breath, with a heartfelt sigh.

C.D.

My voice. Only my voice. You don't need to see
me. Just listen to me. I know I only have a few
minutes here to talk to you. I was wondering if
what I wrote to you touched you. . . .

ROXANNE

It did. It was eloquent.

C.D.

Not eloquent. Just honest. You see, I am in orbit
around you. I'm suspended weightless over you
like the blue man in the Chagall, just hovering,
hanging in a delirious kiss. Yesterday, on the street,
I swore I heard your name. I swore I heard someone say it. And I turned and there was nobody
there, just five birds, and when their wings hit the
air, I heard your name again. And just for that
second, I was one of them, pounding out your
name. Roxanne. Roxanne. The word of two syl-
lables, locked inside my head. You see, I am, and
always will be, the one who loved you without
limits.

CHRIS

What? Too much!

ROXANNE

Go on. . . .

CHRIS

It's working. Go on. Go on.

C.D.

This is my whole life right now, standing here, talking to you like this, saying things I've wanted to say but couldn't.

ROXANNE

Why couldn't you talk to me?

C.D.

I was afraid of having you laugh at me.

ROXANNE

That's so silly.

C.D.

No. Not if you knew. When you're reaching for a star, there's a long way to fall. I almost never let this moment happen. And now all the feelings I'm having that I wanted to give you in a bouquet, I'm throwing them at you in a clump. I love you, I've breathed you in, I am suffocating, I am crazy, I can't go on; it is too much.

ROXANNE

I'm starting to feel a little dizzy. . . .

I'm starting to feel a little drunk. Because you're trembling up there and it's me who has made you that way. And you are trembling, aren't you?

ROXANNE

Like a leaf on a tree.

CHRIS (*shouting*)

I want to make love to you!

C.D.

Shut up, Chris!

ROXANNE

What?

C.D.

I'm telling myself to shut up; I've gone too far.

ROXANNE

I'll tell you when you've gone too far.

CHRIS

She wants us. Look, C.D., it's okay. Sooner or later. You can do it. Come on.

C.D. realizes he's right.

C.D.

Roxanne, don't think I don't know you. Don't think I haven't felt you beneath me. And I know you've imagined it, lying back into your bed with me. You have, haven't you?

ROXANNE

I have.

C.D.

There will never be another tonight, Roxanne. Why
should we sip from a teacup when we can drink
from a river? There is one word, Roxanne. A tiny
word. Not a verb, not a noun, not an adjective. But
if I heard you say it tonight, all this blackness
would go away, and we would be connected by a
tunnel of light.

ROXANNE

What is the word, Chris?

C.D.

Yes.

ROXANNE

I don't know. . . .

Long deliberation.

ROXANNE

All right. All right. Yes. Come up.

C.D. moves as though to, then realizes he can't. Instead, CHRIS
climbs the house, whispering to a surprised C.D.

CHRIS

Thanks! I think I'm in love!

He is gone. The speed with which it has all happened numbs
C.D. In a flash, he has gone from speaking to her directly, to

watching someone else claim his prize. C.D. steps back, looking toward the window, speaking to himself.

C.D. (to himself)

God, I did it.

C.D. stands outside her window, at first watching them kiss, and then, as the lights dim, realizing fully what is about to happen.

C.D. (alarmed)

Shit. I did it!

EXT. STREET—NIGHT

SOPHIE, NINA, DOTTIE, and LYDIA charge down the street. Suddenly, C.D. falls out of a tree and lands flat on the ground.

C.D.

What? Where am I?

LADIES

It's C.D. . . . !

C.D.

Where am I?

DOTTIE

You're in Nelson.

C.D.

Oh God! Oh, thank God! (He kisses the ground.) What day is it?

NINA

It's Friday. . . . Dallas is on.

C.D.

Friday? Then it took no time . . . it didn't exist in time.

LYDIA

What?

C.D.

Maybe it didn't happen. Maybe I was dreaming!

SOPHIE

What happened?

C.D.

I was walking along, and suddenly a spacecraft appeared. It got closer and closer. Then it landed right in front of me! Oh, it was too horrible.

He weeps and wails.

NINA

Tell us.

DOTTIE

I read about this in the *Enquirer*. Did it have lights on it?

C.D.

Lights? You never saw so many lights! It was like Broadway! Then the door opened. A creature came out. He had big suckers on his palms. He walked like this. . . . Then he took his palms and put them right on my face. Took me over to Roxanne's house. Said they wanted to observe them.

LYDIA

At Roxanne's house?

C.D.

That's where they are right now.

LYDIA

This is bullshit. We're going to miss *Dallas*. Let's
go.

C.D. (*crazy*)

You think I'm nuts, don't you?

LYDIA (*scared*)

Uh . . . no.

C.D.

They said they wanted to ask me about older
women.

NINA

Why?

C.D.

Because, they wanted to have sex with them.

DOTTIE

Where?

C.D.

Here! Right here in Nelson! They said they wanted
to start a colony of supermen, who would have sex
with older women, because they really know what
they're doing—

                              DOTTIE
We do!

                              SOPHIE
It's been so long. . . .

                              LYDIA
Two minutes to *Dallas*.

They hesitate.

              LYDIA (*the voice of reason*)
Girls, are you telling me you believe there are
creatures from outer space with big penises who
want to have sex with older women? Let's go check
it out.

They head toward Roxanne's.

                              C.D.
Good night, ladies.

EXT. TOWN MALL—DAY
CHRIS and C.D. help finish preparations for Octoberfest opening.
The MAYOR and DEAN take their places on the small podium. CHRIS
whispers to C.D.

                              CHRIS
God. I was so nervous last night. Uncomfortable.
Believe me, I didn't say anything. I was too dumb
for that. Smart, I mean smart.

                              C.D.
What do you mean you were nervous? How
nervous?

                    CHRIS
Real nervous.

                    C.D.
Real nervous?

                    CHRIS
Yeah.

            C.D. (*hopefully*)
You mean so nervous that you couldn't . . . ?

                    CHRIS
Man, this is embarrassing.

                    C.D.
No, no. Go on.

            CHRIS (*struggling*)
I couldn't do it the third time.

C.D. is crushed. A whistle blows. We are tight on mayor's face.

                    MAYOR
Let Octoberfest begin!

We see down the street. Barely anyone turns. The people who
do mutter, "What'd he say?" We see that DEAN is by the mayor's
side. Having done his duty here, he mutters:

            MAYOR (*disappointed*)
Let's get on over to the barn. This goddamn town.
Shit . . . can't get anything going. . . .

EXT. FIRE STATION—DAY
ROXANNE hurries across the forecourt and into the station.

INT. FIRE STATION—DAY

ROXANNE bursts in. She sees C.D. going up the stairs.

> ROXANNE

C.D.!

> C.D.

Hi.

> ROXANNE (*excited*)

I'm catching a plane in twenty minutes.

> C.D.

Why?

> ROXANNE

The comet. I was right. They called from the
University of New Mexico confirming it. I'll prob-
ably be gone a week. I wanted to tell you first.
You're the one person who could appreciate it.

> C.D.

I'm very happy for you.

> ROXANNE

Is Chris around?

> C.D.

No. I don't know where he is.

> ROXANNE

Would you tell him where I am?

> C.D.

Sure . . . sure.

ROXANNE

And ask him to write me. Tell him I want him to knock me over. Okay? Here's the address. (*Then*.) I was walking on air and now I'm walking on feathers, on pillows, on air.

She hugs him good-bye.

INT. DIXIE'S CAFE—DAY

CHRIS and CHUCK sit at the bar. We drop in mid-conversation.

CHUCK

Gone? For how long?

CHRIS

A week or so.

CHUCK

Whoa, that must be rough on you.

CHRIS

Yeah, yeah it is.

CHUCK

Can I tell you something? I've had a lot of chicks. Between you and me, five figures. But this one's rare. She's smart, she's beautiful, she's a lethal combination.

CHRIS

Yeah, it's a little scary.

CHUCK

I should be so frightened. Listen, I adore this girl. But I'll tell you something about me, maestro. This volunteer fireman knows when he's in over his

head. She'd have me in cement before the week's
up, so I backed off. You're the maestro. You got
the baton. Swing it.

CHRIS nods a sickly agreement.

INT. COW BARN—DAY
We see the cow installed in the barn with a burning lantern
next to it on a stool. The mayor's idea. There are signs around
it to the effect, "On this spot, one hundred years ago . . . ,"
etc.

                         C.D.
    You can't have the lantern.

We see CHRIS and C.D. starting at the mayor.

                        MAYOR
    What? It's nothing without the lantern.

                        CHRIS
    I got news for you. It's nothing with the lantern.

                         C.D.
    No, look, you can't have it.

                         DEAN
    This is unbelievable. Oh man. . . .

                         C.D.
    Use a paper cutout. With little burning flames on it.
    Use a hologram. Anything. You can't use a lantern.

                        MAYOR
    The best-laid plans . . .

He is like a disappointed child. The MAYOR takes C.D. aside.

INT. 279 BAR—DAY
It's early. CHRIS sits at one end of an empty bar. SANDY waits on
CHRIS behind the bar.

> SANDY
>
> Beer?

> CHRIS
>
> Yeah, thanks.

> SANDY
>
> Draught?

> CHRIS
>
> Yeah, but it's okay. I'll just put on my sweater.

Thinking CHRIS really meant this as a joke, she finds it wildly
amusing and laughs heartily.

> SANDY (*laughing*)
> God, that's funny. We get so many guys in here,
> no sense of humor, no sense of humor at all. I
> think a sense of humor is really important. Could
> you hand me those cards over there?

She indicates a deck of playing cards on the counter.

> CHRIS
>
> Sure.

> SANDY
>
> Okay. One hand of lowball for your drink.

CHRIS

What's lowball?

SANDY

You try to get the worst hand.

CHRIS

Oh. Okay. A lowball for a highball.

This devastates SANDY. She laughs riotously.

SANDY

You're a riot.

CHRIS shuffles the cards, rather expertly, and deals them out.

SANDY (*continuing*)

You could be a dealer in Vegas. I know because I
went to Tahoe with a girlfriend of mine and we're
moving there in three days. See, they like young
cocktail waitresses there and you can make big
money. I heard one girl got a ten-thousand-dollar
tip from a gambler that got lucky. Then, when I get
older, I can move to Reno where they like older
cocktail waitresses, and it's only sixty miles away.
What do you got?

CHRIS

A nine, a three, a seven, a five, and a two.

SANDY (*laughing*)

Oh God, that's the worst hand I ever saw! You win.
Where you from?

CHRIS

Albuquerque.

SANDY

A-l-b-u-q-u-e-r-q-u-e. It's an old bar bet. Really?
You know where I really want to go? San Fran-
cisco.

CHRIS

I've been there.

SANDY

You have? You really have? What's it like?

CHRIS (*gets excited*)

It's great there . . . and I'm really a 49er's fan . . .
not so much the Giants though. And the redwoods
are fantastic. I just love to go there and just be. I
always take a meat sandwich with me when
I go.

SANDY

I think it's so great that you've traveled. You're
really interesting.

CHRIS

I . . . I . . . try to be.

SANDY

I think if one person finds another person interesting, then they're interesting to that person. You see
Roxanne, don't you?

CHRIS

Well, kind of. But not . . . not . . .

SANDY

I better quit talking to you. She's sort of a friend of
mine.

CHRIS

No . . . no . . . that's okay. We can talk.

There is contact between them.

SANDY

Okay. (*Then.*) Next you're going to tell me you've
been to New York.

CHRIS

I have. . . .

SANDY

Jeez, I was kidding and you really have!

CHRIS

My name's Chris.

SANDY

I know. I'm Sandy.

CHRIS has met his equal.

EXT. C.D.'S HOUSE—WINDOW—NIGHT
Through the window we see C.D. at his desk.

INT. C.D.'S HOUSE—NIGHT
C.D. sits in his apartment, finishing off a bottle of wine. He takes
a bird from its cage and places it on his nose.

C.D.

Do you love the little birdies so much that you give
them this to perch on. . . .

He empties out his pockets and discovers the note with
Roxanne's address on it. He sits and begins to write her.

EXT. STREET—DAY

C.D. walks down the street past a mailbox. He guiltily checks his letter, then mails it.

MONTAGE

A different day. C.D. mails another letter.

CHRIS supervises the firemen, who are screwing up the hose-drying routine. A hose is stuck. TRENT steps on railing, grabs hose, and disappears. ANDY comes up through frame.

Last, different day. He mails another.

INT. ROXANNE'S HOTEL ROOM—DAY

ROXANNE relishes a letter.

EXT. STREET—DAY

MONTAGE

C.D. puts in another letter.

There is mayhem as the firemen continue the hose-drying training.

INT. DIXIE'S CAFE—DUSK

C.D. sits at a table alone, writing. ANDY and RALSTON in background. DIXIE approaches.

> DIXIE
>
> What's up?

> C.D.
>
> Fine. I mean, nothing.

> DIXIE
>
> Want anything, a drink?

C.D.

All right. But if I ask for more than one glass, give
it to me.

DIXIE

Ralston! Could you bring us a bottle of wine
please?

RALSTON emerges from the back room wearing a waiter's apron.

RALSTON

Yeah.

DIXIE drags out a chair and sits.

DIXIE

What can you sit on, sleep on, and brush your
teeth with?

C.D.

Huh?

DIXIE

It's a riddle. What can you sit on, sleep on, and
brush your teeth with?

C.D.

I don't know.

DIXIE

A chair, a bed, and a toothbrush.

C.D.

What's the point?

                              DIXIE
The point is that sometimes what you should do is
as plain as the nose on your face . . . and in your
case that's real plain.

C.D. is riled.

                              DIXIE
Oh, knock it off. You should tell her.

                              C.D.
Tell who what?

DIXIE leans closer to C.D.

                              DIXIE
You should tell Roxanne that you love her.

                              C.D.
Look, she's not the kind of person . . .

                              DIXIE
She's not what?

                              C.D.
She's not the kind of woman who would want . . .

                              DIXIE
You don't know what women want.

                              C.D.
I told her. Well I sort of told her. Last week. Actually I made love to her.

                              DIXIE
Great!

                              252

C.D.

Well, it wasn't exactly me. It was kind of me. I
was the one who said all the right things, who
made her feel right. It just wasn't the actual me
who made love to her. It was the sort of me.

DIXIE is completely confused, stunned even. CHUCK, wearing
firemen's gear, enters.

CHUCK

This is the deadest place I've ever seen.

He goes to the counter. C.D. looks curiously over at CHUCK.

C.D. (*continuing, to Chuck*)

Hey, Chuck. How come you're in uniform. You're
supposed to be off tonight.

CHUCK

Chris asked me to stand in for him. Roxanne
called around six. Said she was coming in tonight.
He picked her up at 6:30.

C.D.

I didn't tell him about the letters.

DIXIE

Charlie . . . (*Hands C.D. his jacket*).

Panic crosses C.D.'s face. He rises in panic and exits the restaurant.

EXT. DIXIE'S CAFE—DUSK

C.D. tears out of the restaurant and exits.

INT. DIXIE'S CAFE—DUSK

DIXIE sees the letter that C.D. has left on the table. She picks it up for him, to put it away, but she can't help herself. She begins to read it. She is flushed.

Then puts it down. She picks it up. Reads again. Her eyes tear. She puts it down, picks it up, again. She stands up and paces, still reading. She stops and clutches it to her chest. Reads again. Stops. Uses it as a fan while turning small circles. She checks the signature. Then finally just stops: an idea forms.

EXT. ROXANNE'S HOUSE—DUSK

C.D. runs up to the outside of Roxanne's window. He looks up and sees her and CHRIS outlined in the upstairs bedroom. Desperate, he runs to the front door and rings the doorbell. He runs back to the window to see who answers it. We can faintly hear ROXANNE say, "I'll see who it is." C.D. climbs up the side of the house.

INT. ROXANNE'S BEDROOM—DUSK

C.D. enters the bedroom and confronts a confused CHRIS.

> CHRIS
>
> What???

We hear Roxanne's footsteps coming up the stairs.

> ROXANNE (v.o.)
>
> There was no one there. . . .

He dashes out the window and down the side of the house, narrowly avoiding ROXANNE.

EXT. ROXANNE'S STREET—DUSK

Outside the house, C.D. nervously paces. He thinks about it for a moment, then runs to the front door again and rings the doorbell.

INT. ROXANNE'S BEDROOM—DUSK

ROXANNE and CHRIS hear the doorbell again.

> ROXANNE
>
> What is going on?

She starts to go but CHRIS, thinking it's C.D. again, stops her.

> CHRIS
>
> No . . . Let me get it.

He exits the bedroom and goes down the steps.

EXT. ROXANNE'S HOUSE—DUSK

C.D., having rung the doorbell, runs around and climbs the house again, thinking CHRIS is waiting for him.

INT. BEDROOM—DUSK

ROXANNE steps out into the hall just long enough for C.D. to enter the room.

> C.D. (*whispering*)
>
> Chris?

He hears Roxanne's voice just outside the door. He freezes in fear.

> ROXANNE (*v.o.*)
>
> Who is it, Chris?

EXT. ROXANNE'S HOUSE—FRONT DOOR—DUSK

CHRIS looks around earnestly for C.D.

> CHRIS (*shouting*)
>
> Uh . . . I'm looking. . . .

INT. ROXANNE'S HOUSE—HALL—DUSK

She goes back in the bedroom.

INT. ROXANNE'S HOUSE—BEDROOM—DUSK

She swings the bedroom door open; we see C.D. hidden behind the door. The door stops micro-inches away from his nose. CHRIS enters.

>   CHRIS
> Just kids probably.

ROXANNE stops and stares at CHRIS. CHRIS looks around for C.D. but doesn't see him. Something is coming.

>   ROXANNE
> I want to know you. I want to know the side you don't show me.

>   CHRIS
> Huh?

CHRIS turns. He sees C.D. behind the door.

>   ROXANNE
> Do you know why I came back early?

>   CHRIS
> There goes that doorbell again!

>   ROXANNE
> There wasn't a doorbell.

>   CHRIS
> Yes. I heard it. You should answer it.

ROXANNE

There was no doorbell.

CHRIS

I'll get it then.

INT. HALL—DUSK

He starts to go down the stairs. ROXANNE reluctantly follows.

INT. ROXANNE'S ROOM—DUSK

C.D. dashes out the window.

INT. HALL—DUSK

They march down the stairs.

ROXANNE

Chris, there wasn't a doorbell.

The doorbell rings.

CHRIS

There it is again. I'll get it. This could be trouble.

A breeze blows through Roxanne's bedroom door, blowing papers down the stairs. She runs back.

INT. ROXANNE'S BEDROOM—DUSK

She closes the now-open window.

EXT. ROXANNE'S FRONT DOOR—DUSK

C.D. finally confronts CHRIS.

C.D.

Don't look surprised if she mentions more
letters . . .

CHRIS

What do you mean?

C.D.

You wrote her a few letters than you thought. . . .

CHRIS

I did? How many.

C.D.

Three a day.

CHRIS

Three a day. She was gone six days. Six times three
is eighteen.

C.D.

Well, twenty.

CHRIS

Twenty?

C.D.

Or so.

INT. ROXANNE'S BEDROOM—DUSK
CHRIS enters the room to a waiting ROXANNE.

CHRIS

Kids . . . damn kids.

ROXANNE

Chris, when I left, I was ashamed of myself.

CHRIS

Why?

ROXANNE

You know why I came back early? Every day, every hour, you sent me something new. I couldn't stand it anymore. I had to see you.

CHRIS

It was just a few letters, that's all.

ROXANNE

Think of what you wrote.

CHRIS

Uh . . . I'm trying.

ROXANNE

I want to know the real you. The one you're keeping from me.

CHRIS

No . . . not the real me.

ROXANNE

Not that side of you. The one I spoke to the night at that window.

CHRIS

This *is* me. You know, good ole' me. I like hangin' out. Mixin' it up. I like lifting weights. I'm really into my body.

ROXANNE

There's no need to hide yourself any longer. I understand what you're doing and it's not neces-sary anymore. It's what's in here I'm in love with.

She points to his head.

CHRIS

Couldn't I just be cute?

ROXANNE (*advancing on him*)

Don't you see? It wouldn't matter even if you were ugly.

CHRIS

No. . . .

ROXANNE

I want you to teach me what you know.

CHRIS

I can play guitar a little. . . .

ROXANNE

I want to travel with you.

CHRIS

I hate pasta.

ROXANNE

I want to go to concerts with you.

CHRIS (*delighted*)

Yeah . . . boogie.

ROXANNE

New Mexico's going to let me use the telescope. We could go there.

CHRIS

I owe money in New Mexico.

ROXANNE

And we can talk, Chris. We can talk. . . .

CHRIS

I think I'm going to be sick. I gotta go . . . !

ROXANNE stares, disbelieving.

CHRIS

I gotta go. . . !

He runs out the door.

EXT. ROXANNE'S HOUSE—DUSK

CHRIS races out of the house. After a moment, we see DIXIE coming down the road. She walks up to the porch and slides C.D.'s letter under the door.

EXT. SANDY'S HOUSE—DUSK

CHRIS runs out. SANDY has just finished loading her car; her bags are packed.

SANDY

So, are you coming or not?

CHRIS

Yes.

SANDY

You gonna tell her?

CHRIS

I can't. . . .

SANDY

You've got to. It's not nice.

CHRIS

Got any paper? I could write it. I've got a lot of experience at that.

SANDY

I'll get you some.

She exits, and we see CHRIS sit down to struggle with the letter.

EXT. ROXANNE'S HOUSE—NIGHT
We see CHRIS and SANDY pull up and slide a letter under Roxanne's door.

INT. FIRE STATION—NIGHT
C.D. bounds in.

ANDY

Roxanne called. She sounded . . . weird. She said if I saw you to ask you to come over.

He bounds out.

EXT. ROXANNE'S HOUSE—NIGHT
C.D. approaches her house. ROXANNE, anticipating his arrival, opens the door. She is distraught. Her face aches with confusion. They go inside.

INT. ROXANNE'S HOUSE—FRONT PORCH—NIGHT

ROXANNE

Charlie . . .

C.D.

What is it?

She hands him a letter.

Read this.

He nervously opens the letter and reads it aloud.

C.D. (*reading*)
"Dear Roxanne: I've met somebody else and she's
real cute, too. I hope I haven't hurt you but I
probably did. It was really great knowing you and
now I'm going to be a dealer in Tahoe. Yours truly,
Chris."

ROXANNE
And then, I found this along with it under the door.
Read it.

She hands him the last letter he wrote to her. He starts to read it
silently.

C.D.
Uh, huh.

ROXANNE
Read it out loud.

ROXANNE walks in front of him. She cannot see him, only hear
him.

C.D.
"All day long I think, where is she? What is she
doing now? Occasionally I see you on the street,
and I feel the nerves in my stomach, a wave
crashing over me." It's so him.

He stops reading. She turns.

Go on. . . .

C.D.

". . . I remember everything about you. Every move,
no matter how insignificant it might seem. July 11,
2:30 in the afternoon. You changed your hair. Not
that much, but I noticed. And it was as though I
had looked at the sun too long. I could close my
eyes and see it again and again . . . the way your
hair moved, your walk, your dress, everywhere I
looked."

ROXANNE turns and sees that C.D. is moved.

C.D. (*continuing*)

". . . there is a word now that means everything to
me. . . ."

They are now directly on the spot where C.D. spoke to her at
her window.

C.D. (*continuing*)

". . . a word that is the earth, the air, the fire, and
the water. . . . And that word is a name, and the
name is Roxanne."

He stops and recovers.

ROXANNE

It's nice, isn't it?

C.D.

Yes. He . . . writes from his heart.

ROXANNE

Finish it.

C.D.

I did.

ROXANNE

No, read the rest.

He looks over the letter, finding the last part.

C.D.

"C.D. wrote this. Call me. Dixie."

ROXANNE

I looked at all these letters, Charlie. They're all in
the same hand.

ANGLE ON C.D.

He stands rooted on the spot, afraid to move.

ROXANNE

That was your voice that night. . . . Chris didn't
write those letters, you did.

C.D.

Yes. . . .

ROXANNE

All this time, right there in front of me, and I
couldn't even see you.

She walks over to him, slowly, romantically, and slugs him in
the nose!

You bastard!

C.D. (*holding his bleeding nose*)
This is like Niagara!

ROXANNE
How could you do it? How could you trick me?

Then they begin to speak and argue simultaneously.

C.D.
Trick you? I wasn't trying to trick you. I was trying to make you feel good.

ROXANNE
You can't play with me like that. You son of a bitch, you bastard. You played with my emotions.

C.D.
I didn't play with you . . . you could have figured it out. . . .

ROXANNE
So now it's my fault. . . .

C.D.
As much as it is mine. The signatures didn't even match the letters.

ROXANNE
If you're getting love letters, you don't go around trying to match the signature with the handwriting. . . .

C.D.
That's because you wanted to believe it! You wanted it all, the love, the emotion, and all wrapped up in a cute little nose and a cute little ass.

ROXANNE
Goddamn it, you even got me in bed.

C.D.	ROXANNE
Yeah, what about that? You went to bed with him on your first date!	I only went to bed with him because you seduced me! I would never have gone to bed with him.
C.D.	ROXANNE
Well, you still went to bed with him awfully fast. . . .	I don't even consider that I went to bed with him!
C.D.	ROXANNE
Well, somebody was up there, and it's for goddamn sure it wasn't me.	Well, if it wasn't you, who was it? Chris couldn't have seduced me!
C.D.	ROXANNE
This is the very point I was making to Dixie. . . .	You told Dixie? You bastard!

She starts beating him about the face and neck.

ROXANNE

You son of a bitch. . . .

C.D.

I'm warning you, I'm very tough. I could hurt you . . . ow . . . ow. . . .

ROXANNE

How could you have lied? How could you have said all those things?

C.D.

Lie? I wasn't lying! I was telling you how I felt about you.

ROXANNE

If you felt that way, you sure have a lousy way of
telling someone. Just get out of here! Get out of
here!

C.D.

Wait a second. I am out. You get in.

ROXANNE

No, get out.

C.D.

Get in!

ROXANNE

Get out!

C.D.

Go on, get off this porch!

After she leaves

C.D. (*continued*)

And don't try throwing my hat at me.

She throws it.

C.D.

You want to know what the rest of the letter said?
It said, P.S., I was only kidding.

She storms into the house. C.D. stands alone outside, near the
same spot he was the first night he met her. There is a long wait.
He watches the house. He picks up pebbles and throws them
easily against her window. More time goes by. He calls up to
her.

                              C.D. (*shouting*)
        Ten more seconds and I'm leaving. Ten, nine,
        eight, seven, six. . . .

ROXANNE emerges from the upstairs balcony.

                                ROXANNE
        What did you say?

                                  C.D.
        I said, ten more seconds and I'm leaving.

                                ROXANNE
        Oh.

She starts to go back inside.

                                  C.D.
        What'd you think I said?

                                ROXANNE
        I thought you said, "Earn more sessions by sleeving."

                                  C.D.
        Well, what the hell does that mean?

                                ROXANNE
        I don't know. That's why I came outside.

She goes back inside. Something overcomes C.D. His head turns.
He gets a peculiar look on his face. He walks toward the street.

INT. FIRE STATION—NIGHT
C.D. enters the station. The place is unusually tidy and the men
are all busy. C.D. is surprised.

C.D.

Everything okay?

DEAN

Yeah. We just came in to tidy up. . . .

ANDY

Hey, Chris came and got all his stuff.

C.D. stops him with a peculiar look on his face, then turns and exits the station. The firemen follow him out into the street.

EXT. STREET—NIGHT

C.D. stands in the street. His nose sniffs the air. The firemen stand behind him curiously.

C.D.

There's a fire.

The firemen react.

C.D.

There's a fire somewhere. Get the truck.

The firemen run into the station and within seconds they come out with the truck loaded.

ANGLE ON C.D.

The truck follows him as he walks slowly down toward the main street.

ANGLE ON C.D.

As C.D. and the truck pass "All Things Dead," he suddenly speaks.

C.D.

It's the stable!

270

My cow! Great. Another idea ruined.

The MAYOR becomes a sulky child again.

C.D.

If this breaks through to the gas station, the whole
town could go!

EXT. STABLE—NIGHT

The men stand dumbfounded as it appears C.D.'s nose has let
them down. Suddenly, smoke pours from every opening in the
stable and the men, now thoroughly trained, expertly unroll hoses
and hook up equipment. They amaze themselves and they scare
us with their proficiency.

INT. STABLE—NIGHT

It doesn't look like much from the outside, but inside the place
is deeply shrouded in smoke. Flashes of flame leap out occasionally. The men fly to the rear of the stable, where they spot
the cow trapped by the flames. Out of the smoke we see faces
of the firemen emerge and recede. Sometimes we see the cow.

FIREMEN

Mooo. . . . Here Bossy. . . .

The FIREMEN variously plunge into the flames and rescue it in a
surprising display of skill and bravery.

MONTAGE: STABLE

Various shots of the fire being extinguished.

INT. DIXIE'S CAFE—NIGHT

The fire is out. The FIREMEN are at Dixie's celebrating their victory. Everyone is there, including the FOUR ELDERLY LADIES. It's a

real gala event, lots of townspeople toasting, etc. DIXIE distributes flaming drinks.

C.D. enters. He walks up to his firemen.

>   C.D. (*continuing*)
>   You're all real goddamn firefighters now.

Everybody raises their drinks.

>   DEAN
>   To us real goddamn firemen. We beat this fire by a
>   nose!

The place falls instantly silent. A cow moos.

>   C.D.
>   Well said! (*To Dixie.*) I want to see you.

>   MAYOR
>   A toast! A toast! I would like to say that I would
>   rather be with the people in this town than with
>   the finest people in the world!

DISSOLVE

EXT. ROXANNE'S HOUSE—NIGHT

INT. ROXANNE'S BEDROOM—NIGHT

ROXANNE walks by her bed, thinking and pacing.

EXT. DIXIE'S CAFE—NIGHT

C.D. leaves, saying good night to DIXIE.

>   DIXIE
>   What are friends for?

EXT. STREET—NIGHT

C.D. walks home, passing the roof that Peter Quinn was on.

EXT. C.D.'S HOUSE—NIGHT

The camera pans up the house to reveal C.D. sitting on the roof.
There is a big, empty silence.

> ROXANNE (*V.O.*)
> . . . It was as though I had looked at the sun too
> long. I could close my eyes and see it again and
> again . . . the way your hair moved, your walk,
> your dress, everywhere I looked.

At first we think it's C.D. recalling her letter. But we see it's not.
It's ROXANNE in the street.

> ROXANNE
> . . . *your* eyes, *your* face, the way you walk, your
> style, your wit, and your nose, Charlie.

> C.D.
> It doesn't quite work, does it?

> ROXANNE
> I went home and I thought what it was about Chris
> that attracted me. And it wasn't the way he looked,
> it was the way he made me feel. With him, I felt
> romantic, intelligent, feminine. But it wasn't him
> doing that to me . . . it was you. All these other
> men. They've got flat, featureless faces. No charac-
> ter, no fire, no nose. Charlie, you have a big nose.
> A beautiful, great big flesh-and-bone nose. I love
> your nose. (*Then.*) *I love your nose, Charlie.* I love
> you, Charlie.

There's a pause.

ROXANNE (*continuing*)

Well?

C.D.

Are you kidding?

C.D. stands up, and with a grand flourish, slides feetfirst down the roof, bounces off the porch awning (or whatever we decide is convenient), and hits the ground. He stands before her. He starts to kiss her but his nose is in the way. She takes his head in her hands, tilts it sideways, and they kiss. The clouds part; a dashing little slip of a comet appears over their heads.

THE END